U3q

The Dark Kingdoms

Books by
ALAN SCHOLEFIELD

Novels

A View of Vultures
Great Elephant
The Eagles of Malice
Wild Dog Running
The Young Masters
The Hammer of God
Lion in the Evening

History

The Dark Kingdoms

The Dark Kingdoms

The Impact of White Civilization on Three
Great African Monarchies

Alan Scholefield

HEINEMANN : LONDON

William Heinemann Ltd
15 Queen Street, Mayfair, London W1X 8BE
LONDON MELBOURNE TORONTO
JOHANNESBURG AUCKLAND

First published 1975
© Alan Scholefield 1975

Passages from *Congo to Cape, Early Portuguese
Explorers* by Eric Axelson are reprinted by
permission of Faber and Faber Ltd.

Printed in Great Britain by
Cox & Wyman Ltd,
London, Fakenham and Reading

For
Brian and Birgitta
Barrow

Contents

List of Illustrations

Introduction

AT ONE time Africa was a land of many kingdoms, stretching north to south, east to west. There were those that were little more than tribal chieftainships holding a few hundred people in feu, but others were great and flourishing, with long histories, and a pageantry that matched the pre-Renaissance courts of the West. Some of the powerful kingdoms lasted well into the nineteenth century when, having withstood for centuries the attacks of their neighbours, they were finally destroyed by the white invaders who changed the face of Africa.

Although each kingdom collapsed in its own particular way the struggle for survival was often long and bitter. Some kings, sensing they had come into contact with a technologically more powerful people, decided to co-operate; others, afraid of being swamped by inexplicable and alien customs, withdrew into the heartland of their countries and fought savage wars of attrition. It did not seem to matter which philosophy was adopted towards the arrival of the whites, the end was nearly always the same.

But there was a third category: the few kingdoms which survived the white colonial era either because of their remoteness or their poverty or their astuteness.

This is the story of three kingdoms. Two of them succumbed to white pressure and disappeared. One of them survives. Each is seen at a critical period in its history, when black met white head-on.

There is no better example of a country welcoming a white race as friend and ally than the Old Kingdom of Congo on the arrival of the Portuguese. Congo, or Kongo (not to be confused with the modern Congo) flourished in northern Angola in the sixteenth century. Under its most famous king, Affonso I, it went to extraordinary lengths to adopt Portuguese culture and religion, and this period might have been a watershed for a multi-racial Africa had Portugal's greed and militancy not wasted the kingdom internally.

Dahomey, by contrast, was a kingdom that tried as best it could to keep its own identity. Forced to trade in slaves for survival, its kings attempted to keep all contact with whites to the sea coast while they themselves held court fifty miles inland at the capital of Abomey. For more than 250 years a succession of kings allowed few travellers to penetrate the country. But it was only a matter of time before the Dahomean army, with its famous brigade of female warriors, was fighting white forces in a last, vain attempt to save the kingdom.

The surviving kingdom, now with a constitutional monarch, is Lesotho (Basutoland) which still miraculously exists, completely surrounded by South Africa. Its critical period spans the life-time of its founder, Moshesh, who not only withstood attacks by black armies, but also a war with Britain and two wars with the Boers.

Not the least of the factors on which the fate of the dark kingdoms depended was the *kind* of white people who arrived from Europe. What must the citizens of the Old Kingdom have made of a Christianity whose representatives preached on Sundays and slaved for the rest of the week? What can Dahomeans have felt about a Britain that sent Richard Burton, a man who made no effort to conceal his contempt for them, to put pressure on them to change the customs and traditions on which the kingdom was founded?

Moshesh was lucky. The first whites he dealt with made up a small group of French Protestant missionaries who arrived in South Africa with an intense desire to give, wanting nothing in return. Their arrival, a few years ahead of settlers hungry for land, gave him enough time to adjust to new philosophies and a different way of life. He was a man of great quality, a visionary as well as a cunning diplomat. His success lay in the fact that he, unlike the kings of Congo and Dahomey, quickly learnt to play the white game of statesmanship; not only learnt it, but was able to beat the whites themselves at it.

PART ONE

'Royal Brothers'

'Imagination reels at the thought of so much grandeur and so much abasement.'
— Armattoe: *The Golden Age of West African Civilization*

A Portuguese caravel

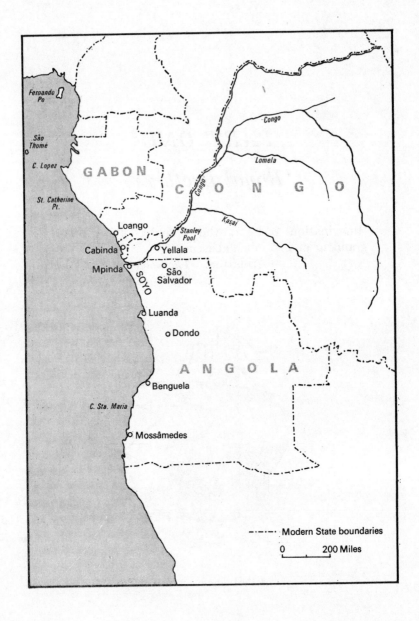

Fernando
Po

São
Thomé

C. Lopez

St. Catherine
Pt.

GABON

CONGO

Congo

Lomela

Congo

Kasai

Loango

Stanley
Pool

Cabinda

Yellala

Mpinda

SOYO

São
Salvador

Luanda

Dondo

ANGOLA

Benguela

C. Sta. Maria

Mossâmedes

-·-·- Modern State boundaries

0   200 Miles

1

WHEN THE Portuguese explorer, Diogo Cão, arrived at the mouth of the Congo River in the early 1480s, Africa south of the equator was as little known as anywhere on earth. Indeed it was not even certain the southern portion of the continent existed. Until a few years earlier the cartographers' world was still that of the *mappamundi*, maps produced in the Middle Ages, based on the Scriptures, often showing the world as a flat disc with Jerusalem at the centre, Paradise somewhere near the top, and the whole surrounded by the great Ocean. Cão had something better to work from. In 1475 a new map of the world was printed but even this, though a great advance over its predecessors and accurate for its day, was unable to speculate on the southern end of Africa.

Cão sailed from the Tagus in 1482 and picked his way carefully round the bulge of Africa into the Bight of Benin and down the west coast. The coastline had already been sketchily explored by earlier Portuguese captains as far south as the present state of Gabon, but once Cão was past Point St Catherine, almost half-way down the Gabon coastline, he was in unknown seas.

Today the big liners sailing between Southampton and the tip of Africa do the journey in less than a fortnight. At most times of the year the seas appear benign, even idyllic; a fresh breeze cools the tropical air, the colour of the water varies between translucent green and deep sky blue. But the farther south one travels, the more dangerous the coast becomes, with icy fogs, contrary winds, shoaling sandbanks and currents that set to the north.

In his recent book, *Congo to Cape*, Professor Eric Axelson of the University of Cape Town, who has made a special study of early Portuguese voyages off the coast of Africa, describes Cão's arrival at the mouth of the Congo the following year: 'From Cabinda to the mouth of the Congo Cão sailed beside a low coastline, luxuriant and green, from which the seabed

3

sloped very gradually, so that the off-shore waters remained extremely shallow; inland rose reddish hills that continued to the mouth of the Congo. At last Cão's ship rounded the point which he called the Cabo das Palmas covered to this day with palm trees and terminating in a rufous-coloured hillock which led later seamen to give it the more colourful name of Red Devil's Point (Ponta do Diablo Vermelho); situated at latitude 5° 44′N, this low cape marked the beginning of the estuary of the great river.'

· The Zaïre or Congo is the third largest river in the world. It drains the centre of Africa and flows three thousand miles before it reaches the sea. More than a million cubic feet of its water enter the Atlantic every second. As the caravel entered the mouth it was dwarfed by the very immensity of the river with its towering tree-lined banks and its maze of islands, some more than ten miles long.

No one has described the river better than Joseph Conrad who went out to it in 1890 as captain of a small steamer. In *The Heart of Darkness* he wrote: 'Going up that river was like travelling back to the beginnings of the world, when vegetation rioted on the earth and the big trees were kings. An empty stream, a great silence, an impenetrable forest. The air was warm, thick, heavy, sluggish. There was no joy in the brilliance of sunshine. The long stretches of the waterway ran on, deserted, into the gloom of overshadowed distances. On silvery sandbanks hippos and alligators sunned themselves side by side. The broadening waters flowed through a mob of wooded islands; you lost your way on that river as you would in a desert...'

As Cão's ship moved slowly upstream the only sound that broke over the dense encroaching bush was the voice of the leadsman calling the marks. They could have had no idea of the importance of the moment. Diogo Cão, a very plain sailor, descendant of a bailiff at the Villa Real in Trasos Montes, was on the threshold of one of the greatest experiments in co-existence between black and white in African history. He was about to start a period that has drawn from scholars such words as 'glorious', 'refined', 'graceful', 'noble'.

Yet, apart from his visit and a mention in Camões' *Lusiads*, written in the middle of the sixteenth century and describing it as 'a river which no ancient knew', the Congo faded from man's interest. In 1816 part of it was explored by a Captain Tuckey of the Royal Navy, but even then nothing much was heard for another sixty years, until the great exploratory journeys of Livingstone and Stanley, when the river passed into modern history.

Cão anchored his ship a few miles upstream and almost at once his crew became aware of figures on the bank. They came down to the water's edge openly and allowed themselves to be taken aboard the caravel where they traded ivory for cloth.

These black people were descendants of tribes which had reached the Congo centuries before in the great migrations that populated Africa south of the Equator. They belonged to a race that had moved away from the cradles of early civilization and had become isolated from the main currents of history and culture. It was probable that they had never seen a white person before and doubtful, so complete was their isolation, that they had ever heard of such people. With Cão's arrival this isolation was to disappear for ever.

'Cão's interpreters attempted to converse with them,' wrote Professor Axelson, 'but could not understand the language, though they did gather that the river itself was called the Zaïre, that it ran through a mighty kingdom called Congo, and that the king of this realm lived a considerable way off in the interior.

'Gathering the impression of a well-ordered society Cão took the risk of asking the local tribesmen to guide to their king a small delegation of Portuguese. He proposed to await their return at an agreed time.'

While he waited he erected a *padrão*—a stone pillar he had brought with him from Lisbon—on which was inscribed: 'In the year 6681 of the creation of the World, and in that of 1482 since the birth of our Lord Jesus Christ, the most serene, most excellent and potent prince, King D. Joao (John) of Portugal, did order this land to be discovered and these *padrãos* to be set up by Dº Cão, an esquire of his household.'

Weeks passed with no sign of the men returning and Cão decided to continue his journey. He made his way a further seven hundred miles south to the present Cape Santa Maria in Angola where he planted his second *padrão* before returning to the mouth of the Congo. The men were not there. He seized four black visitors to the ship and sent a message ashore that they would be returned on his next voyage if his own men were brought safely back. He then sailed for Portugal.

That is how things might have ended, with friendship giving way to animosity, peace to violence. But it did not. Cão did return, not because he specifically wished to exchange the hostages, that was a side issue; he returned because his voyages were part of a pattern by Portuguese and Castilian sailors that were extending the boundaries of the known world. Europe was changing, it was moving out of the Middle Ages into the Renaissance and it had developed a thirst for knowledge.

The pressures to penetrate the unknown parts of the earth were so great that by 1521, less than forty years after Cão's voyage, Dias and Da Gama had opened the sea-route to the east, America had been discovered and the globe circumnavigated.

The particular reasons behind Cão's voyage of 1482–83 and those of Dias and Da Gama later owed much to a mixture of avarice and religious zeal. In sending out his caravels, King John was following the footsteps of his illustrious forebear, Prince Henry the Navigator. News had reached him of great wealth to be found in the interior of Africa and along the western coast; of gold, ivory and slaves. Then there was the question of the spice trade. During the Middle Ages spices had reached Europe from the east by land caravan. But since the fall of Constantinople to the Turks in 1453 the land-routes had become more difficult and more expensive. Cão was attempting to find a sea-route to the east which would give Portugal the spice trade.

There was another reason and it is like a thumbprint of the age: the search for Prester John. It was this, as much as gold and spices, that sent the Portuguese caravels round the tip of Africa. Looking back now on the desperate search for this fabulous monarch one discerns a flavour of Arthur and the Grail. Whether Prester John existed or not there seemed a need at the time to believe in him. Although Christianity was a

6

thousand years old by the time he is first mentioned, the Crusades had ended in disaster and the Holy Places were in the hands of Islam. Christendom itself seemed to be weakening. Superstition was rife; the physical world was not understood and was therefore a dark and menacing place. People clung to their faith and were afraid. Then, in 1145, news of a Christian King living beyond Persia and Armenia, in the depths of the Orient, was brought to the Papal Palace. The legend grew. By 1165 a letter was circulating, purporting to come from this King, who modestly described himself as 'Presbyter Joannes by the power and virtue of God and of the Lord Jesus Christ, Lord of Lords'. It dealt at length with the wonders of his Empire. It was his desire, he said, to visit the Holy Sepulchre with a great army and destroy the enemies of the Cross. He said that seventy-two kings, reigning over as many kingdoms, were his tributaries. His empire extended over the three Indies, including that farther India where the body of St Thomas lay, as far as the world where the sun rose and all the way back again to the ruins of Babylon and the Tower of Babel.

In war, the letter continued, thirteen great crosses made of gold and jewels were carried in wagons before him as his standards and each was followed by ten thousand knights and one hundred thousand footmen. There were no poor in his dominions, no thief nor robber, no flatterer nor miser, no dissension, no lies and no vices. Before his palace was a great mirror erected on a many-storeyed pedestal and by looking at this he could discern everything that went on in his dominions. He was waited on by seven kings at a time, by sixty dukes and 365 counts; twelve archbishops sat at his right hand and twenty bishops at his left.

By the middle of the fifteenth century, this legendary figure had grown in stature; rumour had become fact. Thousands in Europe believed implicitly in his existence. None more so than King John of Portugal. He was a man of short temper, big, bulky and red-faced, who had dealt with an awkward magnate, the Duke of Viseu, by simply murdering him with his own hands. The King foresaw the strategic possibilities of a combined war on Islam, the armies of Christian Europe attacking from the front, those of Prester John from behind;

between them they would crush the enemy But first Prester John had to be found. By the time Cão was voyaging down Africa Prester John was thought to be the Emperor of Ethiopia and the search was drawing to a close.

2

CAO SET off from Lisbon for the second time towards the end of 1485 and the task was the same as before: to turn the southern continent and break into the eastern seas. But in other aspects the voyage was different from the first; this time he commanded a fleet of two or three ships, nor was he any longer a plain 'esquire'; he had been raised to cavalier in the royal household, had been granted a handsome annuity and had been ordered a coat-of-arms charged with replicas of the two *padrãos* he had planted. He had with him, as promised, the four hostages he had taken.

These men, too, were very different from the time they had come aboard his caravel in the River Congo to barter for cloth. They had arrived in Lisbon with Cão at the beginning of 1484 and had spent nearly two years there. Much had been made of them: they had met the king, who was greatly impressed; they had been clothed, converted to Christianity and taught to speak some Portuguese; they had been objects of not unkind curiosity and had been entertained by the nobility. Now they were to be restored to their homeland.

Professor Axelson has said that Cão was given a cordial welcome when the local inhabitants saw he had brought back their compatriots and that they had been well treated. 'According to the chronicler Barros (João Barros, who wrote in the sixteenth century), Cão sent one of the hostages to the King of Congo informing him of his arrival in the river, telling him that the caravels would continue their voyage southward along the coast, and asking that on his return the Portuguese messengers be waiting for him. On their safe delivery he promised to release the three Congolese hostages whom he had still not set free . . . He added that on his return to the river he would seek conversations with the King. Apparently the King replied so promptly that the Portuguese messengers arrived in

8

the charge of one of his captains even before Cão had departed southward; Cão immediately released the remaining hostages and entrusted the Congolese captain with rich presents for his king.'

After journeying up the Congo River as far as the cataract at Yellala where he cut an inscription, he returned to visit the King of Congo at his capital.

Here is Professor Axelson again: 'The chronicler Rui de Pina suggests and Barros insists that Cão went in person to visit the King of Congo and it is likely that (he) followed the old trade route, which in fact was nothing more than a simple footpath, winding its way round boulders, termite mounds and trees, clambering up hillsides, plunging into valleys, seeking out fords to cross the intervening streams and tenuously linking village and village. A later Portuguese official in 1881, when conditions had changed very little from those Cão endured, noted that it took thirty-five and three-quarter hours of actual travel to cover the ninety or a hundred miles from the Congo to São Salvador, by which name the King's city came to be known in the sixteenth century with the arrival of a Jesuit mission. The journey could be covered in five days, but six or seven was more usual, owing to the ardours of the mode of travel.

'Cão's journey, with the armed men necessary to maintain his king's dignity and the native porters needed to carry provisions and gifts for the king and his courtiers must thus have taken the greater part of a week each way. The day's march would start with the light of dawn, and on the first day the stony path switchbacked up and down over a succession of steep and barren hills. In places it crossed great slabs of smooth rock where the booted Europeans had difficulty maintaining their balance, and in the airless valleys the over-clothed Portuguese roasted in the heat reflected from the rocky hillsides. In the late morning the caravan would halt at some village, usually located on a smooth-topped hill close to a source of water, and there, in return for a present of cloth or beads or brass the headman would place a hut at the disposal of the strangers to rest during the heat of the afternoon.

'By the second day the travellers passed into an area of

9

lush forest inhabited by flocks of brilliant red birds with black necks, and on the third day they entered a fertile and populated region which was fed by many streams beside which grew trees with bright scarlet flowers. The narrow path made its way through grass that was often as high as fifteen or twenty feet, and the close walls of vegetation hindered the porters who carried their burdens in bales covered with palm-frond matting. In the early morning the plants were heavy with dew and the travellers were quickly soaked to the skin, so that they envied the naked porters who were spared the discomfort of walking in wet clothes.

'On the fourth or fifth day the travellers crossed the fourth of the steep ridges that lay between them and their destination and descended into the valley of the Lunda, one of the tributaries of the Congo. Since Cão contrived to reach Yellala without mishap in the gorges of the Lower Congo, we can reasonably assume that he was not journeying in the season of the rains, when travel in the Lunda valley is extremely difficult because the rivers are swollen and floods spread over the low-lying ground which can be crossed only by rafts. In the season of low water, the marshes could be crossed by causeways made of tree trunks laid in the water and covered with intertwined branches, and it is likely that Cão and his party crossed the Lunda River, which even in the dry season is a hundred feet wide, by one of the curious suspension bridges, constructed of twisted branches and hung from two anchoring trees, which were a feature of the region: he would probably have been delayed for a long palaver with the local chief or headman who demanded toll at such crossings. Down in the valley the nights were made almost unbearable by the falsetto whining of blood-hungry mosquitoes, whose silent sisters carried the malaria-causing parasites.

'On the last day of the journey the path ascended a steep hillside where a precipice yawned on one side of the travellers; it crossed another wide valley, and then climbed to a ridge of high ground at the southern end of which lay the King's *mbanza*. This capital of the realm of Congo occupied a healthy site, well watered and admirably suited for agriculture, at an altitude of about two thousand feet, between the Luebi and Coco Rivers, looking out over grassland, with the forest in the distance. It was a place that had long been inhabited and cultivated.

'One can imagine Cão and the King meeting in the shade of one of those giant baobab or fig trees which were favoured sites for palavers, with the drums bellowing in the background and soft strains played on horns made out of whole tusks of ivory.'

Cão then sailed south and planted a *padrão* on the coast of the Namib Desert to mark the limit of his voyage. Soon afterwards, for reasons that are not known, he died.

* * *

The next contact between Portugal and the Kingdom of Congo came in 1490. A fleet left Portugal in December and included missionaries, 'secular priests', Franciscan monks, armed soldiers, peasants, masons, carpenters and a few women. They sailed in three vessels which contained, as well as the tools which the artisans would use, church objects and ornaments. There were even building materials. It was a grim voyage. Plague had been raging in Lisbon when the fleet sailed and it had been brought aboard; several of the expedition leaders died.

At the end of March, 1491, the caravels reached the Congo coast in the province of Soyo and were welcomed by the provincial chief, who put on a great show of thudding drums and dancing warriors, and allowed himself to be baptized in the name of Dom Manuel on Easter Sunday.

The Portuguese caravan set off for the City of Congo a few days later. The paths had been cleared and widened and in some parts even swept as though for a royal progress. The more important of the Portuguese were carried on 'wooden horses', poles covered with saddles of oxhide which must have been excruciatingly uncomfortable. It took them twenty days.

At that time, according to an early chronicler, Mbanza Congo was not much more than a dusty bush town. Narrow paths ran in all directions through the tall grass. The huts of the important citizens were close to the King's enclosure, and were of unadorned straw except for the interiors where there were patterned mats. The only distinction between the homes of the nobility and those of the ordinary people was in the size and number of painted mats. And there was the traditional large tree, under which the chief sat to dispense justice. In the centre of the town was a large square on one side of which was the King's enclosure, the circumference of which was about one thousand metres. There were several gates, each guarded by warriors and trumpeters. Then came a second enclosure and a wall of branches which surrounded the palace. It was approached through a maze.

There is a description by the merchant and traveller Duarte Lopez, written towards the end of the sixteenth century after the Portuguese had been there for many years. It seems transformed, with sweet water, fine buildings and churches, a population of 100,000 and a Portuguese quarter occupying nearly a mile of housing. Olfert Dapper, a Flemish traveller who reached Mbanza Congo about one hundred years later, has even left us a sketch of the town. It is built on the top of high river bluffs and has several imposing buildings. A flag on the King's palace snaps in the breeze. Altogether the situation is lofty and airy and must have been a pleasant destination after the wet heat of the Congo valley, which, in years to come, was to kill off so many Portuguese missionaries and traders before they even reached the capital.

When the first great Portuguese mission entered the town in 1491 almost the entire population came out to meet them. Again there was much singing and dancing. The black nobility carried buffalo shields and ironwood swords, the proletariat bows and arrows. It was with this triumphant train that the Portuguese were led to the large huts which had been prepared for them. They were then taken to meet the King, the Mani Congo himself, Nzinga a Knuwu, who was seated on a chair inlaid with ivory and raised on a platform. The visitors came forward with their gifts of brocade, velvet fabrics, lengths of satin and silk, linen, magnificent garments, horse-tails mounted and chased with silver and various trinkets, as well as a cage of red pigeons.

It was an impressive show to a king who was simply dressed in a loin-cloth which had been given him by Cão, copper bracelets and a cap of palm-cloth. The badge of kingship, a zebra tail, hung from his left shoulder. He at once asked to be baptized.

It is difficult to imagine a more auspicious beginning. Here was a powerful monarch in the middle of Africa with no experience of Western ways wishing to embrace the God of his visitors—a God they were importing for this specific reason— almost the moment they arrived. The Portuguese might well have considered this a miracle had a more obvious reason not presented itself. When, a few weeks earlier, the provincial chief of Soyo had been baptized, the Portuguese had completed the celebrations by firing off their muskets in a show of power. Long before they reached Mbanza the Mani Congo had heard of the weapons; seeing them completed his conversion to Christianity. He was hastily baptized John I after the King of Portugal and his wife took the name Eleanor. Various black dignitaries who became known as 'counts', were also baptized, as was the King's son, the 'Duke' of Nsundi. He was given the name Affonso which, as one chronicler has it, 'he was to make glorious'. To round off these sacred ceremonies, building was started on the first church in Mbanza.

It was only then the Portuguese learnt the real reason for the quick conversion; the kingdom was on the point of civil war. Several tribes were rebelling against the central power and the Mani Congo was about to help his son Affonso put down the revolt. Naturally he wanted Portuguese aid. One must try to imagine the Portuguese at this moment: there were not many of them by comparison with their black hosts, they had come to this remote place to proselytize and begin a trading organization—and within a few weeks of their arrival, they were being asked to take part in a war which did not concern them in the least. But the request came from a brother in Christ and it was not possible to refuse. So, a black army marched out on to the central African field of battle under the banner of the Cross, accompanied by a number of white mercenaries carrying muskets. It is hardly surprising that they won the day and returned to the capital in triumph. In gratitude the Mani Congo settled the Portuguese in one section of the town not too far from his own palace and the two races lived in such amity that doors, it is said, were never closed and there was no need for guards. The co-existence had begun.

IT WOULD be hard to imagine two countries more dissimilar than Portugal and Congo at the close of the fifteenth century. Portugal was in the midst of the greatest surge of discovery the world had known and was poised at the start of a colonizing age. The list of her voyages and discoveries in the latter part of the fifteenth and early sixteenth centuries is like a drum-roll: the Cape of Good Hope doubled in 1488, proving that the Indian Ocean was accessible by sea; India reached by Da Gama in 1498; Greenland in 1500; Brazil in 1500; Madagascar in 1501; Mauritius in 1507 . . . and so on. By 1540 the Portuguese empire extended along the coasts of Brazil, East and West Africa, Malabar, Ceylon, Persia, Indo-China, the Malay archipelago, Goa and Malacca.

As the south-westernmost of the free peoples of Europe they were the natural inheritors of the tradition of exploration which had been carried on during the Middle Ages by the Arabs. They began where the Arabs left off by penetrating far into the Atlantic and it was Prince Henry the Navigator who channelled and organized their energy. The compass had been improved and the quadrant and the astrolabe, long used by astronomers, had been adapted for ships so that seamen could establish latitude. Prince Henry placed at the disposal of his captains the vast resources of the Order of Christ (the Portuguese section of the Knights Templar), the best information, the most up-to-date maps.

But as exploration overseas was bringing honour to Portugal the country itself was deteriorating. In mid-century civil war broke out with the Regent, Don Pedro, Duke of Coimbra, leading one faction and the Duke of Braganza the other. In 1449 Don Pedro was defeated and killed and the Duke of Braganza became the most powerful noble in the kingdom, said at one time to own one-third of the entire country. When King John II reached the throne in 1481 he noted acidly that the liberality of former kings had left the crown 'no estates except the high roads'. He crushed the feudal nobility and seized its lands. Ferdinand, Duke of Braganza, was beheaded for high treason in 1483 and a year later the king stabbed to death the Duke of Viseu, his own brother-in-law. For this and other acts he was given the title John the Perfect. He died in 1495 just after his fleet containing priests and presents had sailed for the Congo, and was succeeded by King Manuel I who is known as The Fortunate, because in his reign the sea-route to India was discovered and a Portuguese empire begun.

In contrast to this feverish and thrusting society, the old Kingdom of Congo had been cultivating its own back garden out of sight of the world. At one time it had occupied both banks of the Congo as far as Stanley Pool, but by the time the Portuguese arrived, the Kingdom had shrunk and the capital lay eighty miles south of the river. It was a palm-tree culture. Just as the plains Indians of North America adapted their lives to the buffalo, so did the Bakongo to the palm tree. There were several species of palms which gave the landscape a distinctive appearance and from these the Bakongo extracted oil, wine, vinegar and a kind of bread. The oil came from the pulp of the fruit and looked like greenish butter; they used it for cooking and rubbing into the skin. The bread was made from the kernel of the fruit which, according to Duarte Lopez, was rather like a hard almond. Wine was obtained by fermenting the sap and if allowed to go on fermenting it became vinegar. Lopez says that the wine was drunk fresh 'and is such a diuretic that in this country nobody suffers from gravel or stones in the bladder. It intoxicates when drunk in excess; it is very nourishing'. Apart from sustaining the body the palm tree also gave its fibres for the weaving of mats, baskets, storage containers, clothing, the woven roofs of huts, game traps and fishermen's snares.

The Bakongo knew how to work metals, including iron and copper, and they were fairly skilled potters. They had domesticated several animals—pigs, sheep, chickens and, in some districts, cattle—but unlike most Bantu tribes made no use of the milk.

Apart from the capital, the Bakongo lived in small villages in huts made from wattle frames and mat coverings and travellers would often come on to these villages without warning, for the huts were low and hidden by high elephant grass. Their agricultural implements were limited to the hoe and the axe and they grew a little millet and sorghum. There were bananas and citrus fruits for the picking and an abundance of all kinds of game. Tribal law and custom regulated their daily lives and the witch-doctors had great power. They did not have a written language.

One has the impression of a timelessness which can still be found in Africa today away from the main roads. Enough work is done to exist, no more. As long as there is food and drink ambition is stilled, for the Bantu has never been an acquisitive person. The tenor of life was relaxed, slow, and without worry. Into this calm pond the Portuguese were to toss the doctrine of original sin and moral guilt.

They were particularly indignant at the sexual practices of the Bakongo. In Cavazzi's history of the Old Kingdom, published in 1687, their sins are described as those of 'sensuality or of lust with several women'. At the beginning of the seventeenth century Bishop Manuel Baptista observed angrily that few people 'regard the vices of the senses as sins'. Since many of the missionaries, including monks and friars, had themselves taken black mistresses, perhaps the good bishop was not only fulminating against the Bakongo who were, like many other African tribes, polygamous. Polygamy to the Portuguese meant promiscuity. One writer has managed to trace the sexual appetites of the Bakongo even further and blames the influence of spiced food.

This theme of sexual licence is a constant one in the early writings of missionaries and travellers in Africa and becomes even more widespread, once slavery had begun, as one more way of rationalizing the act of enslavement by disparaging the slave. In fact, Africa was no hot-bed of depravity; on the contrary, there was a rigid morality often amounting to a Victorian sternness. What misled many of the early travellers was the openness with which the African treats sexual matters, the understanding of the need for the sexual release of tension. Among the Zulus, for instance, copulation between unmarried couples was tolerated provided the girl was not deflowered and this led to a form of sexual contact which was safe, but which also gave satisfaction.

Bakongo children were separated from infancy, the boys, as they grew older, sleeping in a place reserved for men, the girls in a separate building reserved for females. Both were instructed by adults in self-control and, as one contemporary Congolese recalls, 'when and how to give in or refuse ... where the-normal-limits of horseplay lay'. The most overt sexual display came in their dances. The partners alternately stamped and rushed towards one another to simulate the sexual act. Once again, like many African dances, these were symbolic of the act of procreation, the natural growth of society. The Portuguese confused representation and fact, symbolic behaviour and licence. One missionary wrote: 'The pen of a devout person refuses to put such things on paper.'

Young people experimented with sex just as young people do everywhere, some experiments went too far, others were more successful. The laws were harsh for the libertine. Promiscuity among young people often resulted in the parties being sold into slavery. Sexual attempts on women returning from work or while bathing in the river carried the same punishment. Masturbation was not looked upon as a vice but homosexuals were severely dealt with. The defloration of a young girl meant reparation to the parents for it was considered that harm had been done to the family. Adultery was considered to transgress religious taboos as well as to cut at the fabric of society itself and for this crime the participants were often wrapped in dried banana leaves and turned into human torches. If their lives were spared they were sold as slaves. It is not surprising that a missionary described adultery as being 'very rare'. Incest was the most heinous of all sexual crimes and was said to cause drought, famine, sudden death, the sterility of women and of the earth.

Sexually mature young men were free to try their charms on the young girls, sometimes they were successful, sometimes not. Occasionally, they might make use of a slave woman owned by a wealthy noble but later on, once the whites had arrived in numbers, prostitution flourished, and then along with the religion, language and culture of the Portuguese, the Congo was to acquire their syphilis as well. The coming of the whites also produced a change in feminine modesty and soon the women were covering their breasts.

But neither the sexual attitudes of the Portuguese nor the changes they brought seemed to make any difference to the

17

warmth with which the Bakongo welcomed them. Historians have been quick to see an affinity between the Bakongo's willingness to adopt Western ways and those of the Japanese 350 years later. But whereas the Japanese wanted the blue-prints of a successful technology while keeping their own religions and customs, the people of the old Congo kingdom seemed to want to *be* Portuguese, at least at the beginning.

4

SOME TIME between 1506 and 1509, the Mani Congo, John I, died. He had, in many ways, been a disappoint-ment to the Portuguese. Quite soon after he had been baptized it became clear that he had become a Christian for reasons of state and he returned to his fetishes and his harem. Traditional elements among the black nobility had never been . happy about his baptism and spoke darkly of ancestors be-trayed, of sorcery and vengeance. But what hastened John's apostasy was the uncompromising attitude of the Portuguese towards his marriages. They saw them as unchristian and tried to bring pressure on him to reject all his wives save one. What they did not realize was that the Mani Congo took on wives for precisely the same diplomatic reasons as European royalty: they represented power blocs. By many careful marriages the Mani Congo was able to make his position virtually unassail-able. When the Portuguese remained intractably moral the Mani Congo reacted: he rejected their religion. About 1495 most of the missionaries and with them certain black nobles who had been converted were obliged to leave the City of Congo. They were led by the king's son who had been baptized Affonso and he settled them in the province of Nsundi well out of the Mani Congo's way. The anti-Christian faction was headed by Affonso's half-brother Prince Mpanza.

The accounts of what happened when the Mani Congo died are rich with romantic legend—and none the worse for that, for they fit snugly into traditional Christian mythology. The story goes that when the king died his wife, Eleanor, allowed no one near his quarters, nor did she release news of his death for three days. During that time she was able to send runners—the

Old Kingdom had developed a fast messenger relay system rather like that of the Incas—to Affonso who, with his small band of Christians, hurried through the bush and suddenly appeared in the city. The death of John I and the accession of Affonso I, as he became known, were announced simultaneously.

But Prince Mpanza now gathered a large army—the number has been given as nearly two hundred thousand—and marched on the capital. Here they were awaited by an army of ten thousand and possibly one hundred black Christians and Portuguese.

From the heights of the City of Congo, the defenders gazed down at the besieging force and many, realizing how badly outnumbered they were, prepared to give up the fight. Affonso told them to trust in God, but their faith must have been weak for they were on the point of deserting when they were checked by the chief of the province of Soyo, one of the earliest converts. This old man is quoted by Lopez as saying, 'Behold my age is now one hundred years and yet I take arms, being zealous for the religion I have adopted, and for the homage and honour I owe to my king, and do you, who are in the flower of your age, show timidity and so little fealty to your lawful sovereign? At least if you will not fight yourselves, animate your vassals, and do not discourage them, but let us await the first encounter with the enemy, and we shall have time after that in which to make plans for our safety.' Then Lopez goes on: 'With these comforting words he reassured the fallen spirits of these men and they turned back with him to seek the king, who was in the church praying and asking help from God.'

On the eve of battle, Affonso's men were greatly heartened by a sudden vision in the sky of five flaming swords. The following day a vision was seen by the enemy; this time of a lady in white, and a knight riding a white horse. When Affonso heard of the vision he sent a message to his half-brother identifying the Virgin Mary and St James, sent by God to defend the right. This was too much for the besieging army; they were routed and put to flight and Prince Mpanza was captured and executed.

Affonso's coronation took place in an open space before the

palace. A low wall separated him from the great crowd that had come to see the ceremony. It must have been a magnificent spectacle. All were dressed in their finest skins and palm cloth, their oiled black bodies shining, the breast-plates of the Portuguese soldiers glinting in the sunlight, the cowled monks in their brown or white habits, the Portuguese civilians in crimson doublets and green hose, and over everything the cobalt blue of the sky, the burning orange sun, the dust rising from thousands of unshod feet.

We have an account of the crowning in 1622 of Pedro II: the throne 'of crimson velvet, all fringed with silk and gold' stood on a magnificent rug. On each side of the throne stood young black nobles holding the royal insignia. One of them had charge of the large Congo flag sent as a gift from the King of Portugal, another held a coat of arms and a third the royal seal. Behind the throne stood a second group bearing the traditional crests of the royal family; these were designs of feathers stuck down on 'curtains of braided straw' hanging from poles six or seven feet high.

There were two other sanctified areas near the throne. One contained an altar stone and crucifix which was symbolic of the King's Christianity. The second was the great royal drum which symbolized his aggressiveness and embodied absolute power. Like all the kings of Congo themselves, who were never permitted contact with the ground and had to be carried everywhere, the drum stood on a piece of ornately woven cloth. It was trimmed with leopard skins and with gold and silver embroidery from which the teeth of rebels were strung. With its grisly relics it was the most dreaded symbol in all the Kingdom and was only displayed on three occasions: a royal death, a coronation, or when the nation went to war.

At a given moment, a melancholy fanfare was repeated twelve times and the coronation ceremony began. First there was a Christian ceremony, brief to the point of abruptness. The King placed his hands on the book of Holy Gospels and swore on the altar to perform faithfully the duties of a Christian king. He was blessed by a priest and that was that. The traditional ceremony, by contrast, was slow and majestic and comprised three parts: the presentation of the regalia, such objects as a small cap of palm leaves and a necklace of iron;

the ceremony of homage in which the important men came forward to kiss the King's hand and pay homage, and then his return to the palace followed by his court.

What sort of man was Affonso I? Here is a priest, Rui d' Aguiar, writing to the King of Portugal in 1516: 'May your Highness be informed that his (Affonso's) Christian life is such that he appears to me not as a man but as an angel sent by the Lord to this kingdom to convert it, especially when he speaks and when he preaches. For I assure your Highness that it is he who instructs us; better than we, he knows the Prophets and the Gospel of Our Lord Jesus Christ and all the lives of the saints and all things regarding our Mother the Holy Church, so much so that if your Highness could observe him himself, he would be filled with admiration.

'He expresses things so well and with such accuracy that it seems to me that the Holy Spirit speaks always through his mouth. I must say, Lord, that he does nothing but study and that many times he falls asleep over his books; he forgets when it is time to dine, when he is speaking of the things of God. So delighted is he with the reading of the Scripture that he is as if beside himself. When he gives audience or when he dispenses justice, his words are inspired by God and by the examples of the saints.

'He studies the Holy Gospel and when the priest finishes the Mass he asks him for benediction. When he has received it, he begins to preach to the people with great skill and great charity, imploring them to be converted and to give themselves to God; in such wise that his people are amazed and we others even more so, before the virtue and faith of this man. Every day he does this, every day he preaches as I have just said. Your Highness will be pleased to learn also that he is very assiduous in the exercise of justice, that he punishes with rigour those who worship idols and that he has them burned along with those idols.'

In other words, Affonso is a *nonpareil*: not only has he learned to speak and read Portuguese fluently, but he has absorbed the faith of his teachers to such a degree that he out-proselytizes the proselytizers. In his study of the Old Kingdom, M. Georges Balandier reminds us that the majority of the documentation is of missionary origin and dates for the most part from the period of militant Catholicism. So that what the Portuguese saw as good they magnified into magnificent; what they saw as bad into abomination.

One of Affonso's first acts on becoming king was to murder a close maternal relative. Some accounts have it that it was his own mother, others that it was her slave. This was a ritual killing. The victim was made to lie on a mat covering an open grave. The mat could not support the weight and the victim fell into the hole. He or she was then buried alive. One theory explains this in terms of symbolism; that the King had to demonstrate in a symbolic manner that he had renounced all family ties, that he had become solitary and was placed over everyone. This may be so but it seems hardly likely that his own mother would have kept her husband's death secret for three days while she sent for Affonso if she knew his first royal duty was to bury her alive. Much more likely is that the victim in this case was Prince Mpanza's mother; a natural choice in the circumstances.

Affonso began his reign as he meant to continue it. The church was as militant then as ever in its history and he fitted well into the pattern. He dealt ruthlessly with those who remained outside it, he destroyed fetishes and symbols of the old worship as far as his power stretched and supplied in their place images of saints, crucifixes, *agni dei*, and other sacred objects. He was also a great church builder and the capital soon earned itself another name, *Ekongo dia Ngunga*—Congo of the Bells. The first church had been built by his father, John I, but rather like John's own faith, had quickly crumbled. During Affonso's reign he built the Church of the Holy Cross before 1517, the church of São Salvador, the most important church in the town, and finally in 1526 the Church of Our Lady of the Victories, known to the townsfolk as *Ambila*, the 'church of the graves', because it was located near the sacred wood where the dead kings were buried. By the end of the century there were six churches in the capital to serve its ten thousand inhabitants. Some were stone-built, others simple affairs of mud and palm matting.

On the face of it, Affonso was behaving in a way his Portuguese advisers could not have hoped for in their most sanguine moments. He seemed to accept everything they told him. On

22

their suggestion he 'ennobled', as his father had done, the principal men of the town, he adopted Portuguese dress and manners and, of course, religion. He sent his sons to be educated in Portugal and kept up a barrage of requests to Lisbon for teachers and artisans. He learnt to read and write Portuguese. He modelled his court after that in Lisbon, established a Portuguese secretariat and imitated Portuguese etiquette. But he was not entirely uncritical. Just as the Zulu kings were appalled at some of the harsh British laws of the nineteenth century, Affonso, who studied the Portuguese code, found that trivial offences often merited grim sentences and he jokingly asked a Portuguese envoy, 'What is the penalty in Portugal for anyone who puts his feet on the ground?'

Perhaps his greatest achievement was his education policy. By 1509 he had built his first school for four hundred pupils; by 1516 Rui d'Aguiar notes the presence in the capital of a thousand students, 'sons of noblemen', who were not only learning to read and write but were studying grammar and the humanities 'as well as the things of faith'. He also mentions schools for girls, a most surprising innovation in Africa, which were directed by a sister of the King.

All this needed organization and, above all, teachers, and much of the correspondence between Affonso and the kings of Portugal consists of pleas for more and more trained teachers. From the beginning of his reign he sent selected young men to be educated at the college of Santo Eloi in Lisbon. Some were his own relatives, some the sons of his new aristocracy. In 1512, for instance, nineteen young men left for Lisbon and in 1516 about the same number.

Not all these young scholars benefited by their new environment but two were to achieve fame. One was to become a professor and finally principal of a Lisbon college; the other, a son of Affonso, was to become a bishop. His name was Dom Henrique, he was eighteen years old and studying in Lisbon when his father decided that he wished to enter direct contact with the Vatican and not go through Portuguese intermediaries as had been the case until then. King Manuel of Portugal made no objection. He was aware that a certain glory would attach to Portugal, not only for discovering the Kingdom of Congo but for having 'civilized' its inhabitants to the point where such a meeting could be feasible; indeed, he went further, he helpfully suggested the protocol for the visit.

It was decided that Dom Henrique would lead the mission, that he would address the Pope formally in Latin and that King Manuel would ask the Pope to create the young Congolese a bishop. While these plans were being formed ships were arriving in the Tagus with ivory, rare skins and palm-cloth textiles for His Holiness and when they had been crated and packed, the strange mission set off across Portugal, Spain, France, over the Alps and slowly down northern Italy towards Rome where it arrived in 1513. Five years later, Dom Henrique was elevated to the rank of Bishop of Utica on the formal proposal of four cardinals, the Papal Bull published by Leo X beginning '*Vidimus quae super Henrici* . . .' Three years later, Henry of Congo returned to his homeland.

It was all very remarkable and in its way very modern; there was the education of students in Europe, the requests for technological aid by Affonso, the concentration on local education, the recognition that the Kingdom was a 'developing nation' and that the quickest way of entering Western trade and commerce was to ape Western methods. Of course the influences and pressures on the Kingdom were enormous. Several fleets set off from the Tagus from 1508 onwards and though many died of sickness aboard the caravels and others of malaria, blackwater and yellow fever once they reached Africa, there were still hundreds of white advisers, priests, artisans, printers, missionaries, teachers and colonial settlers in Mbanza Congo and the surrounding provinces.

In this first quarter of the sixteenth century the affairs of the Kingdom were at the flood. Never again would they be quite the same. The 'royal brothers' of Congo and Portugal treated each other on an equal footing, there was no colour prejudice in the Kingdom itself, the Bakongo yearned to be like their new white friends (not masters), a black king had become a benevolent despot, humane, learned and above all at that time, a devout Christian.

And yet a Roman Catholic missionary in the Congo can write in 1889, nearly four hundred years later: 'A Negro of the Congo knows the names of only three kings—that of the reigning monarch, that of his predecessor, and that of Dom Affonso I.' This is sometimes quoted to reinforce the stature of Affonso and certainly it does, but it poses some equally significant questions: What happened after Affonso? Why were the kings, whose line survived into the twentieth century, so unmemorable? It is as though the last king in French historical memory was Louis XII; in English, Henry VIII.

5

IN A SENSE the experiment in the Congo set a pattern for the future colonization of Africa, for the things that went wrong in the Old Kingdom in the sixteenth century kept going wrong in other parts of Africa until the middle of the twentieth century. Yet, during the reign of Affonso at least, the Portuguese were more humane, more benign, than almost any other Western power that came to occupy a part of Africa. So although much—one could say most—of the blame for what happens next can be attributed to the Portuguese, at least some must be borne by Affonso, who seems to have been a shade too credulous for the good of his own people. He is the kind of African leader one met in the last days of imperialism, the Oxbridge or Sorbonne-educated young man who returns to his people only to find that the gap between them is so wide that neither understands the other. To Affonso's subjects he was still Nzinga Mbemba, but to the Portuguese he was Dom Affonso I; he was the 'father' of his own people, but the 'brother' of King Manuel. It was a schizophrenic relationship.

One of the main reasons why the experiment failed was that Portugal attempted to ship out its institutions unchanged to the African bush. It has been written of the Bakongo that they saw themselves as the central race on earth, that it never entered their heads there could be better countries or better people. The same must hold true of Portugal. To the Portuguese their institutions—church, court, law, education—must have seemed the very best there were, why modify them for Africa?

Unhappily, while some of these institutions blossomed in the mild Atlantic breezes they could not stand the freedom of the boiling African bush. Take the mission of 1508: after sickness had culled the numbers, about fifteen priests, euphoric at being alive, reached Mbanza Congo and offered Affonso grandiose plans for the evangelizing of his people. Affonso was delighted. It was partially for this that he was to keep up his arduous correspondence with King Manuel. But, alas, the good fathers were soon buying and selling slaves, in some cases with funds solicited from Affonso, and setting up house with black mistresses.

Affonso complained to King Manuel and in 1512 received a reply which is one of the most interesting documents in the early history of black and white in Africa. This *regimento* consisted of four sections. In the first it was provided that the Portuguese should help Affonso in the betterment of his kingdom: teaching him how to make war Portuguese-style, instructing him in Portuguese law and court etiquette, and helping him build churches. It also enjoined the Portuguese themselves to act with tact and consideration, to offend no one, but wherever possible to help create an African equivalent of Portuguese society.

The second part was in direct answer to Affonso's complaint against the missionaries. Priests were to live together and were not to accept money from the Mani Congo and those who had behaved badly were to be sent home; any slaves they possessed were to be sent to Portugal at the owner's expense.

The last two sections were frankly commercial. It was pointed out to Affonso that it was not economic for vessels to bring goods to the Kingdom from Portugal and return with empty holds. It was made clear that what King Manuel did for the Congo he did out of love for his brother but at the same time he was not averse to seeing these empty vessels filled up with slaves, copper and ivory on their journey home. Finally, the leader of the Portuguese expedition was to undertake a complete study of the Congo—strength, resources, census— and report back to King Manuel.

In an appendix to the *regimento* the King suggested the titles and armorial bearings—containing among other symbols the famous flaming swords—which the King of Congo should adopt and bestow on his nobility: 'principes, ifamtes, duques, marquezes, comdes, bixcomdes, barões.' The chiefs of the six

26

most important feudatories of the Mani Congo were to be dukes, lesser notables were to be marquises, counts and barons; the King's offspring were to be princes and princesses.

While this document is enlightened for the age—and would have been enlightened at any time during the next three centuries—it contained in it a series of time-bombs, the most important of which was that the local Portuguese were to have 'extra-territorial' rights and were placed under a *Corregedor* or magistrate who tried them according to Portuguese law. Offenders found guilty were sent back to Lisbon for punishment. And so, from the Bakongo point of view, the two most vital factors in law were absent, that justice should be the same for everyone and that it should be seen to be done.

In the event, no one paid much attention to the *regimento*, other than Affonso. Mbanza Congo was what these days would be called a wide-open town and the pickings were too good. Priests traded in slaves, Portuguese adventurers arrived, in spite of Affonso's protests African mistresses moved in with their white lovers and a revolt by a coffle of slaves being taken to Mpinda (the port of the Old Kingdom) caused a flare-up of smouldering resentment. Affonso appealed again to his 'brother' in Portugal.

More than twenty of Affonso's letters to King Manuel and his successor, King John III, survive, and very bleak reading they make. As with Theodore, Emperor of Abyssinia in the nineteenth century, whose letters to Queen Victoria were ignored for years at a time, so it was with Affonso and the Portuguese Court. But where Theodore reacted by imprisoning most of the missionaries and diplomats in his country, Affonso turned the other Christian cheek and sat down once more with secretary and writing materials to chide his brothers for lack of interest.

'Most high and most powerful prince and king my brother,' he wrote to King Manuel in 1517. 'It is due to the need of several things for the church that I am importuning. And this I would not probably do if I had a ship, since having it I would send for them at my own cost.'

The ship is a recurring request. Off the coast of Gabon was the Portuguese island of São Thomé which had been discovered in 1490 and which rapidly became a haven for remittance men, ex-convicts and adventurers. It also became a kind of central slave *entrepôt* and slaves were either shipped on from there or remained to work the island's sugar plantations. Its strategic position as a staging-post to the East, its safe anchorages and its prosperous sugar industry gave the island economic advantages which the Congo kingdom did not have, and Affonso soon found that he was not so much a partner of the Portuguese kings as a vassal of São Thomé.

Even Affonso's son, Dom Henrique, Bishop of Utica, first black bishop of the Kingdom, who had achieved so much simply by becoming a bishop, found his office shorn of authority. He became an auxiliary of the Bishop of Madeira and took his instructions through São Thomé. His life must have been bitter. He was ordered by his father to remain in Mbanza Congo where his false position drew laughter from a white priesthood, itself squabbling over slaving transactions and young black girls. Henrique died in 1535, having achieved almost nothing.

Again Affonso appealed to Lisbon, citing São Thomé's avarice. 'Most powerful and most high prince and king my brother, I have already written to you several times of my need for a vessel . . .' But the São Thomé lobby at Manuel's court was too powerful and no ship was ever allowed to fall into Affonso's hands. At this time all slaves coming from the Congo provinces had to pass through São Thomé whose Portuguese governor, ruling the island like a Roman proconsul, seized a quarter of the slaves for himself. This meant that the financial return Affonso expected was much reduced. In desperation he wrote to King Manuel asking that São Thomé be given to him in fief. He also asked for more teachers and priests. The last lines of this letter read: 'And we beg your Highness not to leave us unprotected or allow the Christian work done in our kingdom to be lost, for we alone can do no more.'

Lisbon was amused at his unworldliness; the King did nothing. Interest was now beginning to swing away from the Old Kingdom and to centre on São Thomé, on the colonization of Brazil, and on the huge empire Portugal had built up after rounding the Cape of Good Hope. By the time King John III began to rule Portugal at the end of the second decade of the sixteenth century, interest in Congo had turned to apathy and the king left Affonso's requests for doctors and technicians unanswered from one year's end to the next.

6

THERE was one factor above all others that bedevilled relations between Affonso and Portugal, and that was slavery; not so much the act itself but the fact that a close connection grew between missionary and slaver, often fusing him into the same person. Africa was no stranger to slavery, in many parts it was indigenous and had been from time immemorial. New pools of slaves were created in familiar ways; by war, by raids and by breaking the laws of a tribe, but it was possible to sell oneself into slavery for strictly commercial reasons. If any slavery can be called benign, that which existed in Africa before the whites arrived could perhaps be so described, and it must have been somewhat similar to that which Wilfred Thesiger describes on the Trucial coast as recently as twenty years ago, where he found African slaves occupying places of great responsibility in the ruling hierarchy. That was all to change for the worse.

In 1442, at a time when the Portuguese were exploring the Atlantic coast of Africa, one of their captains, Antam Gonsalves, who had captured a group of Moroccans and brought them to Lisbon, was ordered by Prince Henry to return them to Africa. He received in exchange for them ten black slaves and a quantity of gold dust. From that moment the fate of millions of black Africans was sealed. Portugal immediately fitted out fleets of vessels, built forts on the West African coast and went into the business of slaving.

It is impossible to say how many blacks were shipped as slaves during the following four hundred-odd years but if one takes the numbers who arrived on the other side of the Atlantic and adds to that the estimates of those who died or were thrown overboard in the middle passage, and again adds the estimated number of Africans killed in slaving raids, the figure runs very high. In his book *Black Mother*, Basil Davidson writes: 'So far as the Atlantic slave trade is concerned, it appears reasonable to suggest that in one way or another, before and after embarcation, it cost Africa at least fifty million souls. This estimate may be about one fourth of black Africa's approximate population today and is certainly on the low side.'

As soon as the real business of slaving got under way, the slave himself became totally subhuman in the minds of the shippers. He was so much flesh and bone which had to occupy the smallest possible space on board ship. The view taken of him on landing was little different. He was a work cypher. This meant that the *kind* of slavery itself had changed: it was no longer the domestic slavery or vassalship understood in Africa, but the cold chattel slavery of Europe where a man was stripped of all his rights and property.

Most people—that is, of those who cared one way or the other—rationalized their guilt. We find that the character of the black man is attacked not only by lobbyists for the slave trade but by intellectuals. Blacks are turned into fiends—cannibalistic, subhuman, sexually gross—in order to 'justify' their treatment. Here is a Liverpool pamphlet of 1792: 'Africans being the most lascivious of all human beings, may it not be imagined, that the cries they let forth at being torn from their wives, proceed from the dread that they will never have the opportunity of indulging their passions in the country to which they are embarking?' There is a need to turn the black man into an *Untermensch* so that what happens to him is of less consequence. The next step is that all blacks are *Untermenschen* and we are racing full tilt towards racial discrimination and *apartheid*.

It did not take long, once the trade really got under way, to find these attitudes widely held. Father Cavazzi wrote in 1687 of the Kingdom of Congo: 'With nauseating presumption these peoples think themselves the foremost in the world ... They imagine that Africa is not only the greatest part of the world, but also the happiest and most agreeable ... '

After the middle of the seventeenth century, most people who were not making a profit out of the slave trade felt it to be morally wrong. Almost every European nation was engaged in it, each excusing itself by depicting the Africans as hopeless savages, at the same time blaming each other for treating them badly. The Dutch said the French were cruel, the French said the English were brutal and that the Portuguese were not only cruel but incompetent. The English made fun of the French for being excitable and of the Portuguese for baptizing whole shiploads of slaves before taking them to Brazil. Malcolm Cowley, in the introduction to his book, *Black Cargoes*, which he wrote with Daniel Mannix, says: 'In truth these wholesale baptisms must have been ludicrous affairs, yet they are not without meaning. They showed that the Portuguese at least regarded Africans as human beings with souls to be saved ...' He adds: 'In the end it is hard to assign the chief guilt to any national group. English, French, Dutch, Danes, Brandenburgers, Portuguese, Mandingos driving slaves from the Niger to the coast, the absolute kings of Dahomey, Yankee skippers, Congolese middle men, and Egbo merchants in old Calabar: the trade brutalized almost everyone who engaged in it. The guilt for it rests not wholly on the white race, or partly on the African kings and slave merchants, but beyond that on humanity itself, the same humanity that was responsible for Auschwitz and Mauthausen and, in its blundering fashion, for Hiroshima and for the next catastrophe; I mean on the apparently inexhaustible capacity for greed and numbness of heart and the infliction of suffering that survives in the nature of man.' The last sentence could be the epitaph for the Old Kingdom of Congo.

7

THE ECONOMY of the Kingdom was based partly on slavery, and the longer the Portuguese remained the more important it became. In the early years other sources of revenue—textiles, ivory and skins as well as dues and tolls—fortunately brought the kings of Congo a lively revenue. Without this money the Kingdom would not have reached the level of development it achieved during the sixteenth century. There was one other source of wealth which was a royal prerogative: the ownership of the source of all currency. They used seashells found on the island of Loanda, which the Portuguese called the *Ilha do Dinheiro* (Isle of Money). Women mined the shells and graded them into sizes with special sieves. All belonged to the King and much went into the pockets of the large numbers of clergy he supported, as well as his masons and artisans who, in fact, did little to earn it. Both sections used the shells to buy slaves.

In the early days of co-existence, the Kingdom's domestic market functioned well. The necessities of life were abundant and there were few manufactured goods that were not common to everyone. If they yearned after any single commodity it was salt and this they prized above most things and paid highly for it.

There was also a ready market for textiles, forged iron and necklaces, but this all changed when the Portuguese brought with them the results of their own technology. Soon red parasols, gilt mirrors, brass hairpins and a dozen other trinkets were displacing the familiar adornments which had suited the Bakongo for so long. They lusted after the new goods. But the Portuguese shipowners in Lisbon had no use for baskets of shells; they wanted 'hard' currency: slaves.

The slaves of Congo occupied much the same position as they did in other parts of Africa; they were workers and servers. But they were also what might now be described as secretaries and factors and in many cases had considerable freedom, journeying on trading missions into the interior on behalf of their owners. This was not what the Portuguese foresaw for their blacks and as their hunger for slaves increased—ironically whetted by Affonso himself, who had sent lavish gifts of slaves to the Portuguese court—the King became more and more isolated in his attitudes.

The export of slaves increased quickly. In the first hundred years of contact the Kingdom was drained of about half a million people. Almost all the Portuguese in the Kingdom were involved. They wanted to be in and out of Congo as fast as possible, they wanted 'instant' fortunes, for they knew that the longer they remained, the less their chances were of ever leaving the place. Here is a contemporary description contained in a letter: 'The climate is so unhealthy for the foreigner that of all those who go there, few fail to sicken, and of those who sicken, few fail to die, and those who survive are obliged to withstand the intense heat of the torrid zone, suffering hunger, thirst and many other miseries for which there is no relief save patience, of which much is needed, not only to tolerate the discomforts of such a wretched place, but what is more, to fight the barbarity, ignorance, idolatry and vices, which seem scarcely human but rather those of irrational animals.'

The traffic began to cause dissension and real fear of depopulation. Affonso must have considered a break with Portugal, but it was not really possible. His own throne was insecure. Several of his vassal states were on the edge of rebellion—largely because they too were being denuded of inhabitants—and it would only need Portuguese encouragement to push them over. Affonso would then have Portuguese arms and armour against him. He stopped short of a complete break and to protect his own people he set up a slavery commission in 1526 consisting of three chiefs to make sure that the coffles of slaves being herded to the coast in increasing numbers were really captives from the interior and not free Bakongo He also wrote another letter to Portugal, this time to King John III.

Manuel, big and brutish though he was, had shown some interest in the Old Kingdom; John III, whose reign began in 1521 and who was eventually to become completely dominated by his ecclesiastical advisers, cared nothing at all. The letter from Affonso took on a bitter note. He complained that traders had undermined his own monopoly on which rested much of his power. 'We cannot estimate,' he wrote, 'how great the damage is, because the merchants mentioned above capture daily our own subjects, sons of our noblemen, vassals and relatives . . . and cause them to be sold.' He complained of the depopulation of his country, of the corruption and licentiousness of the merchants, he begged again for priests and teachers, for wine and flour for the Holy Sacrament and made the emphatic statement, ' . . . it is our will that in these kingdoms there should not be any trade in slaves or market for slaves.'

Nothing could have been further from Portuguese ambitions and a later letter of 1539, a few years before Affonso's death, shows that nothing had changed for the better, only for the worse. Still believing in Portugal's institutions, he sent off five nephews and one grandson, two of whom were to be educated there, two in Rome and two prepared for minor holy orders in Lisbon. He begs his royal brother to 'give them shelter and boarding and to treat them in accordance with their rank, as relatives of ours with the same blood ...' Then he asks after a group of twenty young students sent to Lisbon in 1516, ten of whom had been seized as slaves *en route*. 'But about them we do not know so far whether they are dead or alive, nor what happened to them ...' It is callous enough for the Portuguese court to have remained silent about the young men but one also has the feeling that twenty-three years marks a certain dilatoriness on Affonso's part in asking after them.

The results of these appeals were not what Affonso had hoped: Portugal, to safeguard its source of slaves, began to make alliances with Affonso's neighbours, one of which was the country of Dondo to the south, which was ruled by the Ngola, a title which eventually became the name Angola. The Ngola, a tributary of the Mani Congo's, threw off the yoke in 1556, and fought a victorious battle against the Old Kingdom in which Portuguese settlers fought on both sides to defend their investments.

The last decade of Affonso's reign was marked by dissension and corruption. He was an old tired man, forgotten by Portugal, rotting away in the broiling sun of central Africa, surrounded by scheming immigrants who meddled and vied for patronage and favours, for although Lisbon had little thought for him he still exerted some authority in his own capital.

It is difficult to estimate the number of Portuguese resident in Congo in the 1530s. In his book, *Portuguese Africa*, James Duffy says there were 'never more than two hundred white men, enjoying an influence out of all proportion to their number. Their mulatto children became functionaries, agents of the slave trade, lesser members of the clergy. Children of two worlds, they paid allegiance to neither and were as responsible as their fathers for the constant turmoil that beset the Congo.'

This was the situation when, in the early 1540s, Affonso died.

8

ONE OF the many fascinations of the Kingdom of Congo is that one seems to be studying it by time-lapse photography; everything is accelerated. For the first fifty years the state flowered under its two Christian kings, then it began to wither, an infinitely longer and more squalid process. One can recognize the path trodden by so many other civilizations: the arrival of the founding fathers, the struggle to form the state, the sinewy young nation, the golden age of building and Christian conversion, the disenchantment, the corruption, the beginnings of decline, the invasion of the barbarian hordes, the temporary reunification, the longer decline, the attempt to re-create the golden age, the dismal descent into the dark ages ...

On the death of Affonso, there was a violent struggle for succession between two relatives of the dead king, Pedro and Diogo, which Diogo won. Pedro took sanctuary in a church and remained there until he died, twenty years later. Diogo ruled from 1545 and during his time Congo began its long slide into ruin. It was almost forgotten in Europe except as a place to procure slaves. The church, however, still made fitful attempts to cling to the souls of its inhabitants.

In 1548 the first Jesuits arrived, three priests and a lay preacher, and set about trying to put right the wrongs left by their secular and evangelical forerunners. At first their zeal was exemplary: 2,100 baptisms were recorded in four months, three churches were erected, one of which, dedicated to the Saviour, gave the capital a new name, São Salvador. The lay preacher, Diogo de Soveral, set up schools to cope with six hundred children. For a moment, things looked good. But even so coolly intellectual a group as the Jesuits were unable to withstand the temptations and sly corruptions of the hot land and soon they were buying and selling slaves; one priest, Father Jorge Vaz, collected sixty slaves in three years. Five years after their arrival the Jesuit mission departed wealthy failures.

While this was going on São Thomé was asking Portugal to

boycott Congo because, they said, Diogo was abusing the Jesuits as well as robbing slave caravans on their way to the coast. Diogo replied that the Jesuits were guilty of loose conduct and of calling him an ignorant dog (a serious insult). A second Jesuit mission arrived, but by this time Diogo had pushed his Christianity to one side, had taken on an entourage of concubines and was generally slipping back into pagan ways. He forbade his subjects to attend the missionary schools; there was nothing the Jesuits could do but return to Europe.

In 1561 Diogo died and the battle for succession was re-enacted, with different players. The reign of Affonso II, the heir apparent, was brief: he was murdered while at Mass. His murderer was his own brother, Bernardi, who now became king. He himself died in battle with a neighbouring king and was succeeded by Alvaro I, who ruled for nearly twenty years.

Alvaro's reign began on a not very optimistic note: the borders of Congo were suddenly breached by a tribe called the Jaga, whose ferocity and cannibalistic tendencies caused them to be held in terror. As they swept towards São Salvador, Alvaro, with his *duques* and *marquezes*, *bixcomdes* and *barões*, as well as the white population of the capital, fled to the Congo River and took refuge on an island in the middle of the stream, leaving the Jaga to lay waste the kingdom.

So far the story of the Kingdom of Congo has been pieced together from the writings of priests, missionaries and travellers, some with vested interests in promoting a point of view, most writing years after the events they describe. Now a plain English sailor comes on to the scene who, forty years after the Jaga invasion of Congo, was to fight alongside them and who has left a vivid description: *The Strange Adventures of Andrew Battell of Leigh in Angola and the Adjoining Regions* first appeared in the famous collection *Purchas His Pilgrimes* in 1613 and is an account of what happened to Battell in the years following his departure from England aboard a privateer.

He was born and lived as a child in Leigh near Southend when it was a flourishing port. In 1589 he sailed with Abraham Cocke for the Rio del Plata to prey on Spanish vessels engaged in trade with Portugal's growing colony, Brazil. It was a disastrous expedition and Battell was captured by the Portu-

36

guese with four others while foraging for food on an island off the South American coast. Of Captain Cocke nothing more was ever heard. Battell was first taken to Rio and then back across the Atlantic to Angola where he spent nearly twenty years, much of it in the service of his Portuguese masters trading up and down the Angolan coast. Twice he tried to escape and each time was recaptured and flung into prison.

On one of the trading missions in 1600 or 1601, a black chief called Mafarigosat prevailed on Battell and his men to help him in a tribal war. The traders agreed and with the help of their muskets the enemy was, not surprisingly, demolished. But when Battell and the Portuguese and half-castes of the trading mission wanted to return to their ship, the chief refused. He demanded that one of the whites remain until the remainder returned to help him in another war he was contemplating.

Here is Battell: 'The Portugals and Mulattos being desirous to get away from this place, determined to draw lots who should stay; but many of them would not agree to it. At last they consented together that it were fitter to leave me, because I was an Englishman, than any of themselves. Here I was fain to stay perforce. So they left me a musket, powder and shot, promising this lord Mafarigosat that within two months they would come again and bring a hundred men to help him in his wars and to trade with him ... Here I remained with this lord till the two months were expired, and was hardly used because the Portugals came not according to promise.

'The chief men of this town would have put me to death, and stripped me naked, and were ready to cut off mine head. But the Lord of the town commanded them to stay longer, thinking the Portugals would come.'

Battell took to the bush but was captured by the Jaga and taken to their main camp. Had he known who they were he might have considered himself out of a lukewarm frying pan into the blazing fire, for the word Jaga is a corruption of the Bantu word *a yaka* or *va yaka*, 'they fight'. He says he was taken to a place called Calicansamba, which he describes as a 'town' with avenues of baobab trees, cedars and palms. 'In the middle of the town there is an image which is as big as a man and standeth twelve feet high; and at the foot of the image there is a circle of elephants' teeth, pitched into the ground. Upon these teeth stand great store of dead men's skulls, which are killed in the wars, and offered to this image. They used to pour palm oil at his feet. This image is called Quesango, and the people have great belief in him and swear by him; and do believe when they are sick that Quesango is offended with them.'

The Jaga treated Battell well. They had never seen a white person before and of course had no knowledge of arms. He decided to live with them in the hope that their migrations would take them westward to the coast where he might possibly get a ship. But the Jaga were in no hurry. They remained where they were for the next four months, 'with great abundance and plenty of cattle, corn, wine, and oil, and great triumphing, drinking, dancing, and banqueting, with men's flesh, which was a heavy spectacle to behold'.

After more than a year of wandering, the Jaga, accompanied by Battell, did turn westward, attacked an Angolan chief and burnt down his town: 'Here we found great store of wild peacocks, flying up and down the trees in as great abundance as other birds.'

Once again they moved westward and attacked a chief who seven years before had routed a Portuguese–Angolan army of more than forty thousand led by Balthasar de Almeida. The Jaga laid siege to the town and during this time Battell managed to escape. He joined a caravan of slavers and finally reached his Portuguese masters.

In all he was with the Jaga for twenty-one months, living and fighting as one of them. His most valuable asset was his musket and, he says: 'I was so highly esteemed with the Great Gaga because I killed so many Negroes with my musket, that I had anything I desired of him.' His brief descriptions of Jaga social life and habits have stood the test of later scholars.

According to Battell they had a great predilection for palm wine and must have caused much devastation in order to get sufficient quantities, for he writes that they 'cut the palm trees down by the root, which lie ten days before they will give wine. And then they make a square hole in the top and heart of the tree, and take out of the hole every morning a quart, and at night a quart. So that every tree giveth two quarts of wine a

This engraving of São Salvador, capital of the Kingdom of Congo, shows in a somewhat idealized form the progress made by 1686.

The King of Congo, possibly Alvaro, receives a deputation of Portuguese visitors

A Congolese aristocrat using hammock-men for a journey in the bush. Burton was to use a similar conveyance later in Dahomey.

The king's throne and insignia (in the foreground), as Dapper saw them late in the seventeenth century.

Dress and weapons used by the inhabitants of Congo in the eighteenth century.

day for the space of six and twenty days and then it drieth up.'

Here is his marvellous description of the 'Great Gaga' as he continues to call the Jaga chief, Calandula: 'The Great Gaga Calando hath his hair very long, embroidered with many knots of Banba shells, which are very rich among them, and about his neck a collar of *masoes*, which are also shells, that are found upon that coast, and are sold amongst them for the worth of twenty shillings a shell: and about his middle he weareth *landes*, which are beads made out of ostrich eggs. He weareth a cloth about his middle, as fine as silk. His body is carved and cut with sundry works, and every day anointed with the fat of men. He weareth a piece of copper cross his nose, two inches long, and in his ears also. His body is always painted red and white. He hath twenty or thirty wives, which follow him when he goeth abroad; and one of them carrieth his bows and arrows; and four of them carry his cups of drink after him. And when he drinketh they all kneel down and clap their hands and sing.'

One of the oddities of the Jaga was the practice of killing all their own children by burying them alive, while rearing those of their beaten enemies. There are echoes here of the Mamelukes of Egypt who preferred to train Georgian slaves as their successors rather than bring up their own children, of the *arioi* priesthood of Tahiti and even, in some respects, of the Turkish Janissaries who recruited only Christian children. Battell writes that when the Jaga took a town they kept the boys and girls of thirteen or fourteen as their own children.

'But the men and women they kill and eat. These little boys they train up in the wars, and hang a collar about their necks for a disgrace, which is never taken off till he proveth himself a man, and bring his enemy's head to the General (chief); and then it is taken off and he is a freeman, and is called *gonso* or soldier.'

A point on which there is a good deal of speculation is Battell's constant reference to cannibalism, for except in circumstances of great famine as occurred in Lesotho in the nineteenth century, cannibalism in Africa was mostly ritualistic. 'When the Great Gaga Calandola undertaketh any great enterprise against the inhabitants of any country, he maketh a sacrifice to the Devil, in the morning, before the sun riseth. He sitteth upon a stool, having upon each side of him a manwitch: then he has forty or fifty women stand round about him, holding in each hand a *zevra* (zebra) or wild horse's tail, wherewith they do flourish and sing. Behind them are great store of *petes*, *ponges* and drums, which always play. In the midst of them is a great fire, upon the fire an earthen pot with white powders, wherewith the man-witches do paint him on the forehead, temples, 'thwart the breast and belly, with long ceremonies and inchanting terms. Thus he continueth until sun is down. Then the witches bring his *casengula*, which is a weapon like a hatchet, and put it into his hands and bid him be strong against his enemies ... And presently there is a manchild brought before him; two whereof, as it happeneth, he striketh and killeth; the other two he commandeth to be killed without the fort.

'Here I was by the man witches ordered to go away, as I was a Christian ...'

In 1610, Battell returned to Leigh with, as his servant, a young boy who claimed to have been held captive by a gorilla. At that time a Reverend Samuel Purchas was Vicar of Eastwood, a village two miles north of Leigh, and it was he who worked with Battell on an account of his *Adventures*.

9

SUCH WAS the tribe which had sent Dom Alvaro I, the Mani Congo, fleeing to the island in the Congo River with his white advisers and his black noblemen.

The exact island, among the hundreds which turn the river into a watery maze, upon which the Bakongo were to spend about a year, is uncertain. It is sometimes referred to as the Isle of Horses, at others Hippopotamus Island or Elephant Island. We do know that it was small, a factor which was to aggravate an already horrific situation, for plague soon broke out.

The Kingdom itself was devastated. The Jaga entered São Salvador and burnt it, slaughtering anyone who survived. Their army then split into separate regiments and conquered the remaining provinces. Thousands of homeless wandered the roads, many of them dying eventually of starvation. On the island the plague grew worse and was accompanied by a shortage of food. King Alvaro sickened, not with plague, but with dropsy from which he suffered for the rest of his life.

As those on the island reached the edge of starvation slavers arrived from São Thomé with food. The traveller Lopez describes what happened next: 'The price of a small quantity of food rose to that paid for a slave, who was sold for at least ten crowns.

'Thus, forced by necessity, the father sold his son, and the brother his brother, everyone resorting to the most horrible crimes in order to obtain food.' The food was unloaded, the weak, half-dead sons and brothers of dukes and marquises and barons were transferred to rowing-boats and thence carried farther downstream to where the caravels from São Thomé were anchored. Yet even as the slaves were being sold both sides observed the letter of King Affonso I's slavery decree. Here is Lopez again: 'Those who were sold to satisfy the hunger of others were bought by Portuguese merchants ... the sellers saying that they were slaves, and in order to escape further misery, these last confirmed the story.' There can have been few sights in Africa sadder before—or since—than men and women pretending to be slaves so that those actually selling them could benefit by obtaining food.

As the weeks passed into months and things grew worse, King Alvaro turned in desperation to Lisbon. He sent an ambassador to young Sebastião of Portugal and for once a request from Congo was answered with speed. In 1570 Captain Francisco de Gouveia and six hundred soldiers and adventurers reached Congo. He was joined by Alvaro and his rump of courtiers, bodyguards and white settlers and in nearly two years of intermittent fighting, the combined force eventually broke up the Jagas and drove them out of the Kingdom. Afterwards Gouveia built a strong wall around the town of São Salvador. In gratitude for the restoration of his kingdom, Alvaro formally acknowledged vassalage to the King of Portugal and agreed to send annual tribute of one-fifth of the yearly collection of cowrie shells, which could always be exchanged for slaves. He then married, had four daughters and two sons, and an additional two daughters by one of his slaves. He is almost the last great figure in the story of the Old Kingdom.

The Jaga invasion had given the Kingdom a severe shock and once Alvaro regained his throne in São Salvador he was able to take stock of the future. It did not look promising. The Jaga had been defeated, not destroyed, and were perched on his frontiers ready to strike again. Angola, his great southern neighbour, was being opened up by the Portuguese and colonized. He must have felt caught between the two pressures which were to mark African history from that point on, the pressure from within—historically a fact of life and one with which all African kings had had to deal—and that from Europe unfamiliar and therefore frightening. He did what his predecessors had done, the only thing he could do: he appealed to Portugal and Spain (which had ruled Portugal since 1580) and he also appealed to the Pope. He asked for missionaries and artisans to help rebuild his kingdom. He also offered to hand over his copper and silver mines. For years Portugal had been certain that vast deposits of minerals lay in the hinterland of Congo, though no one had discovered them, least of all the kings, so that the mines which Alvaro generously offered to transfer only existed in the imagination.

Alvaro was unfortunate in his ambassadors. One was the Portuguese merchant Duarte Lopez. He left Congo in 1583 with a pouch of letters and a head full of careful instructions. But the ship in which he was travelling sprang a leak near the Cape Verde Islands and was blown by contrary winds to the West Indies. It finally sank off Grenada and the crew and passengers had to swim ashore. Lopez was marooned there for nearly a year before he could join a fleet sailing to Spain.

In the meantime Alvaro, having heard no news and fearing that the ship and his ambassador had been lost, sent off his prime minister, Dom Pedro Antonio, in another ship. This was captured by English pirates. A prize crew was put aboard and the ship sailed for England. As they were landing the ship was wrecked and Dom Pedro and his son, who had accompanied him, were drowned.

By the time Duarte Lopez had recovered from his ordeal and felt well enough to leave Spain and complete his mission to

Rome, King Alvaro I had died and had been succeeded in 1587 by his son, Alvaro II. He knew that his father had wanted to remove Congo from Portugal's tutelage and place it directly under the Holy See and he worked towards the same end. The pressures that Alvaro I had recognized had built up even further, and Alvaro II made repeated efforts to dissociate Congo from the Angolan territories which now were blatantly colonial and whose colonists were trying to nibble away at the borders of Congo. He appealed directly to the Pope, offering 'all the metal which will be discovered in the Kingdom' in exchange for protection against 'force and vexations'.

But poor Alvaro II had as little luck with his ambassadors as his father had. The envoy this time was Antonio Manuel who was robbed at sea by pirates and delayed both in Lisbon and Madrid. He reached Rome on January 3, 1608, four years after leaving Congo and so exhausted was he and so despondent—he had seen most of his embassy die *en route*—that two days after arriving and within hours of delivering his message, he too died. It is by the grandeur of his funeral, which was said to have been the equal of that of a former ambassador from France, that Congo was finally recognized by the Vatican as a Christian kingdom. The funeral was described as one 'almost befitting a king', and there is a fresco in the Vatican showing the Pope visiting Antonio Manuel on his death-bed. But for all the funeral pomp, little was achieved in the way of help for Congo and the following year Alvaro II died without achieving his greatest ambition, the disengagement of Congo from Portugal.

It would be tedious to enumerate the kings that followed him; their reigns were short, their lives filled with rivalry and intrigue. The swift turnover meant that some were only children, like Alvaro IV who came to the throne in 1631 aged thirteen and ruled only four years.

While the various factions were competing for power within the kingdom, great changes were taking place in the outside world. The southern Atlantic, which had for so many years been the private preserve of Portugal and Spain, saw the influx of France, England and Holland. The Dutch began settling in the province of Soyo and entered the slave trade. In Angola the Portuguese allied themselves with the Jaga and raided

Congo for slaves. Things became so bad that King Garcia II Affonso (1641–61) made common cause with the Dutch against the Portuguese and was able to gain some control of his country once more. But in 1648 the Dutch abandoned Angola. They already had their eyes on the Cape of Good Hope, which they were to colonize four years later; Congo was left to the tender mercies of the Portuguese once more.

The King was defeated, a treaty was signed containing punitive clauses, slavery was rife, everything was collapsing. In 1665 came the final ironic blow: two Christian armies, both marching under banners of the Cross, met on the field of Ambouila. One was a black army led by King Antonio I, the other Portuguese. The Bakongo suffered a total defeat and King Antonio was killed and decapitated.

10

AND THAT is almost that. By 1667 the Portuguese had got all they could out of Congo and were abandoning it. A few years later, a bishop was to write of São Salvador that it was nothing but 'a den of savage beasts'. By 1701 a report stated: 'The news coming from the Congo is always worse and the enmities between the royal houses are tearing the Kingdom further and further apart. At present there are four kings of the Congo ... There are also two great dukes of Bamba; three great dukes in Ovando; two great dukes in Batta, and four marquises of Enchus. The authority of each is declining and they are destroying each other by making war among themselves. Each claims to be chief. They make raids on one another in order to steal and to sell their prisoners like animals.'

Almost, but not quite ... there is one surprise remaining which sounds an historical echo so loudly one might almost accuse the Old Kingdom of stage management. And yet it springs surely out of the misery and chaos that made up Congo at the end of the seventeenth and beginning of the eighteenth centuries. Out of the ashes of Christian teachings and the old fetish religion, was born a new cult which took for its banner the golden age of Affonso I; it was a religion born of nostalgia, of distaste and despair for the present, and in that sense it was as much a political revolutionary movement as it was evangelical. The new cult started when a young woman professed to have seen the Virgin and to have learnt of Christ's indignation at conditions in Congo. There is a strong relationship between this revelation and those made to Joan of Arc in France in the fifteenth century and to a Xhosa maiden in south-eastern Africa in the middle of the nineteenth century, which we shall deal with later. The three occasions coincided with periods when the nations to which the mystics belonged were threatened by overwhelming pressures. According to this woman, the Virgin asked her to recite the Ave Maria three times and ask for Divine Mercy three times each evening. A young man took this slightly further by announcing that in his revelation a warning was given that the people of Congo would be punished unless they rebuilt São Salvador. Next an old woman said she had found the head of Christ which had been disfigured by man's sins. This turned out to be a stone brought up from a river. She also claimed to have had a vision of the Virgin.

These were no more than the stirrings of a new religious feeling. The true Joan of Arc figure and the founder of the Antonian sect, which was to sweep the Old Kingdom with the promise of a golden future in the shape of the past, was a young girl of noble birth named Kimpa Vita, who called herself Dona Beatriz. Like Joan, she took up the task of wiping out the evils besetting her country. Here is a description of her by Father Laurent de Lucques, a Capuchin who was to fight her and her new religion with great ferocity. 'This young woman,' he wrote, 'was about twenty-two years old. She was rather slender and fine-featured. Externally she appeared very devout. She spoke with gravity and seemed to weigh each word. She foretold the future and predicted, among other things, that the day of Judgement was near.'

By 1704 her teachings were spreading outwards and she was gaining disciples all over the land. Even what was left of the nobility in São Salvador, where she later preached, gathered to her, touching her and being touched, giving her their cloaks to cover her head, fighting over food or drink which she had touched. When she travelled, the paths were cleared ahead of her by a group of women disciples. When she walked along these paths it was said that twisted trees grew suddenly straight. The word went out that at long last God was coming to the aid of the anguished Kingdom and that Dona Beatriz was His representative.

Father Bernardo de Gallo, another Capuchin, described an interview he had with her in which she revealed the miraculous beginnings of her conversion from heathenism. He wrote: 'She said it happened this way. She was lying ill unto death when a brother dressed as a Capuchin appeared to her. He told her he was St Anthony, sent by God to restore through her the Kingdom, to preach to the inhabitants and to chastise severely those who opposed it.' Thereupon she died but revived when St Anthony entered her body. She told her parents what had happened and set out on her great mission to the capital where she claimed St Anthony was the 'second God' and that he held the keys to Heaven. The sect took its name from him.

According to M. Balandier, in his book, *Daily Life in the Kingdom of the Kongo*, she succeeded in combining the religious tradition of Congo with Portuguese Christian tradition; St Anthony, deeply revered in Portugal, was one of the three saints worshipped in the Old Kingdom. Balandier describes how she tried, symbolically, to revive the beginnings of Christianity and bring about its rebirth. She imitated the death of Christ each Friday, went up to Heaven where she dined with God and pleaded the cause of Congo and was born again each Saturday. She imitated the Virgin and longed to give birth, by immaculate conception, to a new Saviour. And when she did have a son she said to Father de Lucques, 'I cannot deny that he is mine, but how I had him I do not know. I do know, however, that he came to me from Heaven.' Simple words, one might think, even touching, but given the religious fanaticism of the times, deadly.

Dona Beatriz was a revolutionary who would have found a place in any one of several black movements today. Some of her teachings are bizarre enough, but beneath them one can find the first stirrings of *négritude*, of black power, of the belief that black is beautiful. She emphasized the differences between black and white rather than the similarities. White people, she said, came originally from a kind of clayey rock, while black people sprang from the wild fig tree. Her preachings were part prophecy, part political doctrine. She taught, for instance, that Congo was the true Holy Land and that the founders of Christianity were black. She said that Christ was born in São Salvador and was baptized at Nsundi and that the Virgin Mary was the daughter of a black *marqueze* and a concubine. She predicted a golden age when São Salvador would be rebuilt and repopulated and would be filled with 'the rich objects of the whites'. She foretold that the roots of fallen trees would change into gold and silver, that fabulous mines would be discovered containing metals and gems. To be part of this wonderful future all one had to do was believe.

Father de Gallo and Father de Lucques fought her influence by every means at their disposal. Father de Gallo in particular denounced her 'frauds' and said that to lend credence to her powers of divination she had parcels of cowrie shells buried in different parts of the ruined cathedral, then publicly revealed the location of the caches.

But Dona Beatriz was hard to fight because she had modelled herself closely on the missionaries themselves. She preached against vice, superstition, the old fetish religion and in general against the same sins as the good fathers. She adapted the *Ave Maria* and the *Salve Regina*. She established her own church, sent out disciples to proselytize those who lived in the distant areas of Congo and even set up a nunnery. She soon began to be regarded by her black flock as a saint.

While she accepted and preached many of the Christian precepts, she was solidly against the missionaries and their white religion. Her people were told not to worship the Cross because it had caused Christ's death. She rejected the Catholic form of baptism, its confession and prayer, and made polygamy 'legal'. Foreign priests were threatened, discomfited, and accused of opposing the work of salvation of the 'black saints'. As her religion grew, so did nationalist sentiment: Antonianism gave expression to the need of many Bakongo to rebuild their society.

All this was watched with the gravest concern by the Capuchins. They saw Antonianism as a force which would weaken and finally destroy Catholicism in Congo as well as the link between Congo and Europe which was now more than two hundred years old. Since Antonianism was more than simply a religion—it was belief in the future of the nation itself—it was hard to fight. Here is Father de Gallo again writing of the time when Dona Beatriz journeyed to São Salvador: 'Thus it came about that São Salvador was rapidly populated, for some went there to worship the pretended saint, others to see the rebuilt capital, some to see friends, others attracted by the desire to recover their health miraculously, others still out of political ambition and to be the first to occupy the place. In this manner the false saint became the restorer, ruler and lord of the Congo.' Antonianism was all things to all men, but the one thing it did not do was make Dona Beatriz ruler of Congo, as Father de Gallo suggests. Had it done so she would have been safe.

The Capuchins could no longer stand by and watch the erosion of Catholicism by a quasi-religious, nationalistic movement, so they began to put pressure on the Mani Congo, King Pedro IV. For a time the King was unmoved but then, when it became plain to him that his own situation was being weakened by pretenders who were using the new cult against him, he acceded to the Capuchins and had Dona Beatriz arrested. It was within the King's power to have her executed for committing the heresy of claiming her child was Heaven-sent, but he hesitated, the current of popular sentiment was running strongly in her favour. He seriously considered allowing her to escape to her followers. But the Capuchins sensed his indecision and, motivated 'solely by zeal for the glory of God', as Father de Gallo has it, exerted more pressure. The King gave in and his royal council passed a sentence of 'death by fire on the false Saint Anthony and his guardian angel'.

The sentence was carried out on July 2, 1706, and here is Father de Lucques' eye-witness report on the death of Dona Beatriz, for which he shared responsibility: 'Two men holding bells ... stood in the midst of this huge throng and gave a signal with their bells, and at once the crowd fell back and in the midst of the empty space the *basciamucano*, the judge, appeared.' According to de Lucques, he was dressed from head to toe in a black cloak and wore a hat on his head of a black 'so ugly that I do not believe its like for ugliness has ever been seen'. Dona Beatriz, carrying her baby son, was led before him. She appeared to be very frightened. They sat down on the hard ground and waited for the sentence to be carried out.

'We understood then that they had decided to burn the

child along with his mother,' says Father de Lucques, allowing himself a flash of pity. 'This seemed to us too great a cruelty. I hurried to speak to the King to see whether there was some way to save him.'

The judge made a speech which had nothing whatever to do with the matter in hand, being a eulogy of the King, at the end of which he pronounced the sentence against Dona Beatriz, saying that 'under the false name of St Anthony she had deceived the people with her heresies and falsehoods. Therefore the King, her Lord, and the Royal council condemned her to die at the stake together with her child.'

Father de Lucques describes how she made every effort to recant but without success. 'There arose such a great noise among the crowd that it was impossible for us to be of help to the two condemned persons. They were quickly led to the stake ... For the rest, all we can say is that there was gathered there a great pile of wood on which they were thrown. They were covered with other pieces of wood and burned alive. Not content with this, the following morning some men came again and burned the bones that remained and reduced everything to very fine ashes.'

Antonianism did not die suddenly, but lingered on in the shadow of its first martyr. 'Relics' were collected, places at which she had taught were considered holy. For a time there was hope of the kingdom recovering its national vigour. But it was not to be. The pressures had been too great, the greed too widespread; and the Old Kingdom of Congo slipped out of men's consciousness into an age of darkness.

By the end of the eighteenth century São Salvador was a ruined city, its churches tumbling down, its walls open to any marauder. A priest who made the long journey from the coast wrote to the Bishop of Angola that he found only an agglomeration of untidy huts behind a palisade, nothing more. 'It has passed away like the torrential rains which simply moisten the surface and leave the subsoil dry and sterile.' Some years later the Old Kingdom became part of Angola. The last half of the nineteenth century saw a great influx of missionaries in Africa and once again the Old Kingdom seemed profitable ground, this time to the Baptists, who set up a mission at São Salvador in 1878.

In the 1950s São Salvador was visited by F. Clement Egerton, who says in his book, *Angola in Perspective*: 'It has completely lost any romantic character it ever had, and is now no more than a straggling village. The walled cities have disappeared and the eleven churches with them. What is left of the Cathedral is unimposing, just the chancel arch and some low remains of chocolate-coloured walls. It is surrounded by the unkempt grass which is everywhere to be seen in the dry season; and the graves of the early kings of the Congo, rough, obelisk-like monuments in an untidy churchyard, look unkempt and neglected also.'

He spoke to an old man of nearly seventy who sported a magnificent white moustache and who called himself Dom Pedro VII, the last king of Congo, but there were rumours that he was an impostor. He lived near the ruins of the cathedral in an unpretentious house around the walls of which hung copies of paintings of Portuguese royalty.

Egerton was shown the 'regalia' which he describes as 'a royal robe trimmed with white fur, which looked more like rabbit than ermine, a silver crown, a sceptre, and miscellaneous utensils, none of which looked more than a hundred years old. It was rather pathetic.' This old man, who died in 1955, was given a small subsidy by the Portuguese authorities which he increased by growing a little coffee and rice.

Since Egerton's visit a great deal has happened in Angola and much of the country has been convulsed by civil war. On the night of March 14, 1961, a Bakongo terrorist organization called the União das Populacãoes Angolanas (U.P.A.) crossed the northern border of Angola into what had been the Old Kingdom and slaughtered more than two thousand Europeans, half-castes (whom they ceremoniously beheaded) and black contract workers who had come north to work in the coffee plantations. (It was this operation which began the Angolan emergency, the conduct of which was radically affected by the 1974 left-wing *coup* in Lisbon.) The group of terrorists was led by Holden Roberto, who had been educated by the Baptists at São Salvador and who saw himself as the modern king of Congo, before opting for fervid pan-Africanism on the Nkrumah pattern. It has been estimated that most of the deaths in the slaughter that followed were among the contract workers. These came from a people called the Ovimbundu, of whom the Jaga once formed a part. After the massacre, about twenty thousand refugees fled south, many dying of hunger and thirst on the way. It was several years before they gradually returned to their homes.

São Salvador has changed since Egerton's visit. There is a splendid Franciscan mission in the village with a school holding five hundred children as well as a teachers' training college. In 1971 there were four white bishops in Angola, one half-caste, one Goan—and one black. . . .

PART TWO

'The King's Head Thing'

'It is no mere lust of blood nor delight in torture and death that underlies the rite (human sacrifice) in these lands. The King has to perform a disagreeable task over his ancestral graves, and he does it; his subjects would deem it impious were he to curtail or to omit the performance, and suddenly to suppress it would be as if a European monarch were forcibly to abolish prayer for the dead.'
—Sir Richard Burton

Regiment of Dahomey Amazons in action

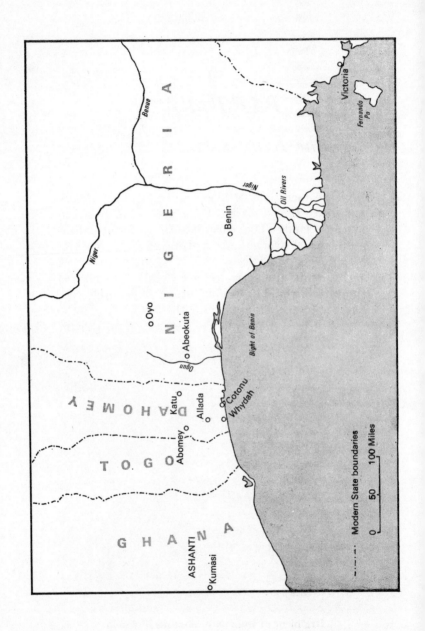

1

UNLIKE THE Old Kingdom of Congo, Dahomey made an impact on the world from an early stage in its development. In an area of Africa which was the very heartland of the slave trade, Dahomey was among the most notorious of all the black slaving nations; and among a group of peoples who practised ritual murder, it was Dahomey which became the most infamous. Of its culture, of its unique dualistic bureaucracy, little was reported and less cared about. While slavery was what might now be called a growth industry, Dahomey was wooed by every white slaving nation; when at last the conscience of the world was aroused, Dahomey was vilified, blockaded and put under pressure to stop the flow of slaves. It can perhaps be said that Dahomey was created by external pressure and finally weakened by external pressure. But unlike the Kingdom of Congo it had an internal strength, a recognition of its own destiny that has assured its survival, true in a different political body, until today. The great difference between the two kingdoms as far as the life-force is concerned is that Dahomey was built by black people while much of the Kingdom of Congo was created by whites.

The beginnings of the Dahomean nation-state are lost in mists and myths. At the start of the seventeenth century there was no such place as Dahomey and it seems to have emerged between 1620 and 1630 when the Fon, a race who lived inland behind the Slave Coast, drew together in self-defence against the slave-raiding of their eastern neighbours, the Yoruba of Oyo and the coastal kingdoms of Whydah and Allada. So in the beginning Dahomey was forced to protect itself against precisely the sort of depredations it was later to practise on others with such economic success.

One other major factor affected the country's growth: its geographical peculiarity. Today its shape is roughly that of a thick but stunted tree which sprouts on the coastline of the Bight of Benin and grows due north into the bulge of Africa between Togo and Nigeria. Its littoral is only sixty miles wide, its length at best four hundred and fifty miles and its widest point about two hundred miles. Until well into the eighteenth century it was much smaller, consisting only of the area around the old capital of Abomey, which lies about fifty miles inland, and it had a population of about two hundred thousand. At that time the Dahomeans, like their inland neighbours, were terrified of the sea; it was tabu. However, unlike their neighbours whose lands were bounded by swamps, mountains, rain forests and wide rivers, the young Dahomey was an almost featureless area of bush country difficult to defend without superior arms, and the most superior arms were flowing into Africa from Europe as payment for slaves. They could only get arms by going to the coast for them. So it was that in spite of this tabu, in 1727 Dahomey broke through to the coast, taking as it did so the small independent statelets of Whydah and Allada which, until then, had refused to allow it to sell its slaves except through them. They were helped by a natural phenomenon called the Gap of Benin, a break in the forest zones lying on either side of Dahomey, which connects the hinterland with the coast giving the country a different climate from that of its neighbours. It is a *lusus naturae*, a freak of nature which is called by the French 'the hole'. Along several thousand miles, from Senegal to the Niger, the hinterland of West Africa is approachable from the sea only at the mouths of rivers, but once through the rough surf off the coast of Dahomey a traveller could walk the short distance to Abomey with relative ease. From the moment they established themselves on the coast, the Dahomeans' power and reputation began to grow. It is also from this period that the world began to notice Dahomey.

As an introduction to the long association of European slavers with the country, one can do no better than quote a letter from the splendidly named Bullfinch Lamb which was written from Abomey in 1724, three years before the breakthrough to the coast. Captain Lamb, an agent of the English African Company, had been captured by the Dahomean monarch, 'Trudo Audati, King of Dahomey and Emperor of Popo' when Dahomey overcame the town of Jaquin, and was taken to the King's court, where he became a much-favoured prisoner. His letter is to his superior in Whydah, Mr Tucker.

From the Great King Trudo
Audati's Palace of Abomey,
in the Kingdom of Dahomey.
Nov. 27, 1724.

Sir,

About five days ago, the king of this country gave me yours of the 1st instant, and immediately required me to answer it in his presence, which I did, though in a very indifferent manner: so that if I do not recall it, I hope you will excuse that as well as this.

As to the late conference I had with his majesty on receiving your letter, I think he does not want to make a price to let me go; for when I pressed him much to tell me on what terms he would send me away, his answer was, he did not want to sell me, I was not a black man; but upon my again pressing him, he made a sort of jesting demand to the sum of I think 700 slaves, about £10,000 or £14 a head. Which strange ironical way of talking, as I told him, made my blood run cold in my veins . . . he is prodigious vain and proud, but he is withal, I believe, the richest king and greatest warrior in this part of the world; and you may depend on it, in time will subdue most of the countries round him. He has already set his two chief palaces round with men's skulls, as thick as they can lie on the walls, one by another, and are such as he has killed in war; each of which palaces are in circumference larger than St James's Park, about a mile and a half round.

After a plea that something be done so that he was not forced to spend his youth 'as it were for nothing in this cursed place', Lamb goes on to say that he is being treated well, that he has been given male and female servants and a constant supply of food and drink to maintain both himself and his staff and that 'if I loved brandy I might soon kill myself, having enough of that'. This is a recurring theme. Many of the travellers who reached Abomey in the following 150 years had to wait months before permission was given to leave, and they record a constant intake of rum, brandy, gin and claret by which they cushioned themselves from the heat, frustration and terrors of the court.

Whenever the King walked in public Lamb was ordered to attend, often having to sit for hours in the harsh sun, though being allowed a 'kidey-soll or umbrella' to prevent sunstroke. For such attendance the King often gave him a reward of cowrie shells, 'two, sometimes three or four grand cabess'.[1]

Lamb became something of a gentleman-in-waiting to the King and whenever His Majesty rode abroad he was ordered to accompany him. He was given a horse but lacked saddlery and in his letter he asks for 'horse furniture' to be sent from the coast both for himself and the King 'as it is very uneasy to ride a bare horse'. He rather touchingly suggests that the company charge him for these things as well as one or two other objects like 'a little English dog' and a pair of shoe buckles which the King needed.

In case the English African Company felt that he was worrying too much about his own fate, Lamb suggested that Mr Tucker send him money so that he could promote the company's interest by trading for slaves while still a captive. He went on:

> Most of the ink you sent me being unfortunately spilt I beg you will send me a paper of ink-powder. His Majesty has likewise got from me the greatest part of the paper, having a notion in his head of a kite, which, though I told him it was only fit for boys to play with, yet he says I must make one for him and I to play with; so I beg you will send two quires of ordinary paper and some twine for that use, and a score of match, His Majesty requiring me sometimes to fire his great guns, and I am much in fear of having my eyes put out with the splinters.

He asked for any prints, pictures or books which Mr Tucker might have handy, for the King had a delight in looking at things like that and often carried a Latin mass-book which he apparently consulted whenever he had decided *not* to grant Lamb a request. Then a most surprising request: 'If there is

---

[1] The existing exchange rate was four boges to one tokey; five tokeys to one gallina; twenty gallinas to one grand cabess, which equalled one pound sterling.

any cast-off woman,' Lamb wrote, 'either white or mulatto, that can be persuaded to come to this country, either to be his wife or to practise her old trade, I should gain His Majesty's heart entirely by it and he would believe anything I say about my going and returning again with more white men from the company.'

He described the battle in which he was captured. The house where he had been staying in Jaquin had been one of the first fired by the attacking Dahomean army. He had lost all his possessions but had managed to get clear and watch the remainder of the assault. He was then captured and taken to the Dahomean general who, 'though he was in a great hurry and flushed with victory took me very kindly by the hand and gave me a dram, which was some comfort to me, though I knew not who he was . . . .' He accompanied the general through the streets of the town where 'there was scarce any stirring for bodies without heads, and had it rained blood it could not have lain thicker on the ground.' Lamb remained in the town for two more days and then was carried by hammock-men into the interior.

Having seen so many cruelties committed on the bodies of old men and women, also on such as were not able to travel by reason of their wounds and burns, etc, I could not choose but labour under dismal apprehensions, particularly the first morning when they led me out, as I imagined to sacrifice me, with a drum beating a sort of dead march before me, and many hundreds gathered about me, jumping and tearing, enough to rend the very skies with such a noise as would fright the devil himself. Many had drawn swords and knives in their hands, which they flourished about me, as if ready for execution. While I was calling on God to have mercy upon me, the general sent orders to the petty captain of war to bring me to him, being retired about two miles out of the camp. His orders were quickly obeyed, and I brought to him, which put an end to my fears.

I should have given you an account of my introduction to the king had not His Majesty sent this minute in a hurry to me for this letter, which I cannot have time to copy or correct, as I intended. I therefore beg you will pardon

tautology and all other faults. Being, with hearty service to
all the gentlemen, Sir, Your most obedient humble servant,
                                        Bullfinch Lamb.

Eventually Lamb was given permission to leave Abomey
and he returned to Britain a much richer man than he had
left. The King of Dahomey had given him a parting gift of
320 ounces of gold and eighty slaves, as well as an interpreter
called Tomo who had also been captured at Jaquin. Two
reasons have been advanced for the King's munificence:
firstly, that he wanted to open communications with King
George I of England and discover as much about Britain as
he could; secondly, he hoped to try and prevail on Whitehall
to stop exporting slaves to the colonies but instead to buy
them and keep them on the Guinea Coast to work at European-
supervised plantations.
    Before Lamb left he was required by the King to take a
most solemn oath to return, but unlike Diogo Cão, whose
honour is one of the small bars of sunshine in the story of the
Old Kingdom, Lamb never did. Nor did he send Tomo back to
report on life in Britain. Instead he went off to Barbados and
sold Tomo to an American. This breach rankled with the King
and it did not incline him to think well of Europeans after
that. It is possible that the incident was kept fresh by the
keepers of the tribal memory for when Richard Burton
visited Dahomey in 1863 he was fulfilling a promise to return
made a year previously during a brief visit to Abomey. The
fact that Burton kept his promise caused the then King,
Gelele, to treat him with exaggerated respect.
    There were relatively few European visitors to Abomey
before or after Burton; had foreigners been allowed to wander
freely about the countryside there would have been many
more. But the virtue of having a capital a good few miles inland meant that any potential traveller had first to get in
touch with the King's viceroy at Whydah on the coast and
apply for permission to visit Abomey. A few travellers and
slavers, among them the Englishmen Robert Norris, Frederick Forbes, Eardley-Wilmot and J. A. Skertchly, did receive
permission and each wrote an account of the visit. But by far
the most important traveller to reach Abomey was Burton. He

was a man with a trained mind, a brilliant linguist, and a writer with endless patience for whom no detail was too small or insignificant. In her essay *Richard Burton: The African Years*, Caroline Oliver writes: 'The most important result of Burton's visit was the book[1] he wrote. It is the best description of Dahomey written while the monarchy was still a living force. It is also probably his best African book, because his interest in, and understanding of much of his subject often surmounts the impulse to jeer. He describes Fon culture and religion, the Dahomean constitution and the sacrificial rites with objective authority, and as usual the detail is astonishing. During the five-day ritual at Abomey, he recorded every dance movement, the pattern of every one of hundreds of decorated umbrellas and every ceremonial wiping of the royal nose and face. As the record of a visit of little more than two months it is a great achievement.' And for all his outlandish statements on race, his rash temperament and his open dislike of Negroes he seems able, in his book, to divorce the scholar from the bigot and gives us the clearest as well as the most detailed picture of the Kingdom of Dahomey at almost the height of its power.

Yet if Dahomey was strong, it had now reached a critical period in its history. After an existence of nearly two and a half centuries in which it had emerged as one of the most powerful kingdoms in Africa, it was, only thirty years after Burton's visit, to be gobbled up by the French Colonial Empire. From early in the eighteenth century Britain had been exerting growing pressure on the Dahomean kings to stop slaving and put an end to the 'Annual Customs', during which Abomey, the capital, reeked with the blood of human sacrifice. It was the British Government, in the shape of Burton, which arrived in Dahomey in 1863 to exert yet more official pressure. To appreciate the meeting between Burton and Gelele, the last of the great Dahomean kings, it is necessary to discover who they were and what had produced them.

[1] *A Mission to Gelele, King of Dahome.*

2

RICHARD BURTON was born in 1821 in England, but a few months later his family moved to central France, and from then on he saw little of England until he was old enough to go to Oxford. His was a remarkable childhood. In an age when children were strictly controlled, he and his younger brother Edward grew up in an atmosphere of such freedom that their self-willed behaviour became a scandal wherever their father settled.

At nineteen, Richard went to Oxford. He was a tall muscular young man with a fierce, drooping moustache and a manner not calculated to bring out affection in his elders and betters. Indeed by the time he was sent down for disobedience, his intellectual arrogance had developed to a point where he was roundly disliked by his professors. He was by this time a steady drinker, a massive smoker, including the occasional pipe of opium, a fine swordsman and a precocious sensualist. He had also developed the passion for languages which was to dominate his life. At Oxford he questioned his tutors' pronunciation of Latin and German, and it is typical of him that when he did at last go to Dahomey, he wrote of it as Dahome, its people, the Fon, as the Ffon, and its capital Abomey as Agbome.

From Oxford he joined the Bombay Native Infantry, as a result of which he spent nearly seven years in India, very few of which were actually occupied in soldiering. He worked on a geographical survey of Sind (which he spelled Scinde), and took part in the regimental sports of boxing, cock-fighting and pig-sticking. Gradually he became so proficient in a few chosen tongues that he found it amusing to disguise himself as a Moslem and wander in places where no ordinary white man would have dreamed of going. He became fascinated by the sexual practices of the Orient, and produced a report on homosexuality in Karachi which he presented to the Commander-in-Chief of the Army, Sir Charles Napier. Later this was forwarded to Bombay where its pornographic details so horrified officials that

Burton became dubbed 'the white nigger', a calumny in his eyes, since he despised Negroes. He was socially ostracized and nearly dismissed the service. All prospect of promotion vanished.

He was bitterly disappointed. Weak from cholera, and suffering from ophthalmia, he sailed for England on extended sick leave, where he launched himself on his literary career with several books on India and Goa. In one he suggested that suitable punishments 'for controlling the natives of Central Asia' might be flaying the men alive, chopping them in two vertically, stoning them to death, impaling them and cutting off their limbs. He also favoured flogging instead of imprisonment, and in this at least he shared an African philosophy; from Gelele in the north-west to Shaka in the south-east, African kings professed astonishment at the cruelty of the prison system practised by the whites.

The next ten years contain everything that made Burton famous in his lifetime. In 1853 he journeyed to Mecca and Medina in disguise; the following year he visited the closed city of Harar where, as in the earlier journey, one false step would have brought instant death. There was a spell in the Crimea from 1855–56 and then came his great Central African journeys: the discovery of Lake Tanganyika, the endless marches, the recurrence of ophthalmia, fever, the conflict with Speke. Once again, by the time he left Africa early in 1859, his health was in ruins.

By 1861, Burton had also visited America and after a stormy courtship of ten years, at last got married. Once more he was short of money, so he began looking round for employment. He decided on the Foreign Office and in particular, fancied the position of consul at Damascus. But his reckless arrogance was beginning to pay reverse dividends. There were too many people in high places who had suffered from him over the years to acquiesce now in his desires. Instead, he was offered the consulship on the tiny island of Fernando Po in the Gulf of Guinea at a salary of £700 a year. It had the reputation of being the graveyard of the consular service. Burton wrote to the Foreign Office accepting the post and the army happily eliminated him from its ranks.

So, at the age of forty, without financial reserves or the

prospect of a pension, he began a new career in Africa, at the bottom of the diplomatic ladder.

* * *

The island of Fernando Po lies off the West African coast less than five hundred miles from Dahomey and Burton was in no hurry to reach it, which was just as well, since the captain of his steamer was on salary-and-commission and the commission was based on the amount of coal he saved each voyage. The result was that the vessel pottered slowly south, first to Madeira and the Canaries, which Burton did not care for, then a succession of West African ports which he cared for even less. The basic reason was that they were inhabited by black Africans and he was not a lover of the Negroid races. His previous experience of Africa was mainly that of the east–central regions, of relatively unsophisticated savannah tribes whose contact with Europeans was limited and in some cases non-existent. In the lake regions it was earliest morning in the relationship between white and black and there was still a pristine quality about it; in West Africa it was late afternoon, and a pretty dismal and tarnished afternoon at that. The blacks on the littoral had been selling their inland brothers for hundreds of years. Sierra Leone was partly populated by freed slaves; so was Monrovia. There was very little you could tell either side about each other they didn't already know.

Burton was shocked when at Sierra Leone a porter demanded double pay for carrying his bag because he would be 'breaking the Sabbath'. He writes dryly: 'I gave it readily and was pleased to find that the labours of missionaries had not been in vain.' And he reflected on 'how much better is the heart of Africa than its epidermis'.

Farther down the coast he was incensed to learn that the term 'nigger' had been outlawed and was equally upset when a few blacks rode as first-class passengers between the ports. 'It is a political as well as social mistake to permit these men to dine in the main cabin which they will end by monopolizing. A ruling race cannot be too particular about these small matters.'

Here is Burton the philosopher on the subject of race: 'I

believe the European to be the brains, the Asiatic the heart, the American and African the arms, and the Australian the feet, of the man figure. I also opine that in the various degrees of intellectuality, the Negro ranks between the Australian and Indian—popularly called red—who is above him. From humbly aspiring to be owned as a man, our black friend now boldly advances his claims to *egalité* and *fraternité*, as if there could be brotherhood between crown and clown! The being who "invents nothing, improves nothing, who can only cook, nurse and fiddle", who has neither energy nor industry, save in rare cases that prove the rule!—the self-constituted thrall, that delights in subjection to and imitation of the superior races . . . And yet we—in these days—read such nonsense pure and simple as "Africa for the Africans".' It may have been as well for Burton's choler that he did not know the Dahomean kings considered themselves so superior to Europeans that they did not deign to shake their hands.

He reached Fernando Po on September 27, 1861, and felt 'uncommonly suicidal' on the first night he spent there. It is hard not to feel sympathy for him. The island had been discovered by the Portuguese in the fifteenth century but ceded to Spain in 1778. First attempts to develop it failed and, with Spain's consent, the administration was taken over by Britain who used it as a base for her West African Squadron which was engaged in suppression of slavery. The main industry was the palm oil trade, the climate was hot and sticky and the coastal regions malarial; yellow fever ravaged the island from time to time; it was not the most salubrious spot.

Burton began the years of Foreign Office employment as he meant to continue them: absent without leave. He was only in the Fernando Po office a week before he was off to inspect the Oil River ports in the Niger delta. Back for another week and then off again, this time with the commander of the West African Squadron, to Nigeria, the Cameroons and Lagos, whence he visited the town of Abeokuta, the capital of the Egbas, the implacable enemies of Dahomey. During the trip into the West African hinterland he must have made his secret trip to Dahomey. It had to be secret because he had applied to the Foreign Office for permission to visit the kingdom and had been refused.

On his return to Lagos he went off to Victoria in the Cameroons where he organized a small mountaineering party and he was so delighted with the trip that he reported back to England on the healthiness of the country; suggesting its suitability for hospitals in which white administrators could recover from fevers and tropical diseases. Actually the Cameroons, with its high rainfall, would have killed them off in shoals. He visited Gabon looking for gorillas, then went to England on home leave, returning to West Africa in 1863. Fernando Po seemed more congenial to him on his return because he moved away from the coast into the hills. Even so he did not stay long but was soon off to explore the Congo estuary, Luanda and parts of Angola. Each of his West African trips resulted in a two-volume book. Apart from *A Mission to Gelele*, he wrote *Abeokuta and the Cameroons Mountains*, *Wanderings in West Africa* and *Two Trips to Gorilla Land and the Cataracts of the Congo*.

It was when he returned from the Congo that the British Government entrusted him with a mission to Dahomey.

3

THE HISTORY of Dahomey has close links with and indeed runs parallel to the expansion and subsequent falling away of the slave trade. By the time the Fon came down through the Gap of Benin to capture the coast towns, Whydah was already established as one of the busiest and cheapest slaving ports; Dahomey had a ready-made business. All it needed was slaves, but no African community sold its own people into slavery unless they had committed serious crimes. So the raiding system began, with the result that nations rose and fell in proportion to their ability to wage war on their neighbours. The long war of attrition between Abomey and Abeokuta, for example, shows first one side in the ascendancy, then the other.

To withstand these attacks, a people needed weapons, to obtain weapons they needed slaves, to raid for slaves they needed weapons: it was a terrible spiral maze through which no nation of the Slave Coast was able to escape. Huge quantities of firearms were poured into West Africa. One estimate gives the number of guns manufactured in Birmingham alone at the height of the slave trade as between 100,000 and 150,000 a year. The saying was: one gun, one slave; though Basil Davidson points out that this was on the optimistic side, since African traders were seldom willing to sell a captive for a gun alone but demanded other goods as well.

The European traders on the coast, who lived in the shadow of forts built by their respective countries to safeguard national slaving interests, might well have regretted the huge inflow of guns, for it strengthened the bargaining power of the African slavers and their factors, the *mongos* and *cha-chas*. But there was nothing they could do about it. They were caught in a dilemma of their own making; they had to have slaves, and to get them they had to pay with guns.

In all this turmoil, one surprising fact emerges and that is the internal stability of Dahomey once it had achieved its enlarged borders. There can be few black states—or white, for that matter—whose kings reigned as securely or for such lengthy periods as those of Dahomey. Gelele, for instance, whom Burton came to visit, was the ninth king of the Alladahonu dynasty at Abomey which had begun just over two hundred years before. If one accepts the kingdom's dates as being from 1650 to 1889 then there were only ten kings and their average reign was twenty-four years. This contrasts with Dahomey's neighbours. At Porto Novo, for instance, the average reign was less than nine years. One of the ways in which the ruling clan of Dahomey managed to avoid the parricide and fratricide that occurred wherever kingdoms flourished was to exclude male descendants of recent reigning kings from important offices and to use the females of the royal household as administrators. The King was always chosen from the ruling clan and his name was given out to the people before his father's death. Long reigns meant late successions for many of these rulers, which in turn eliminated much of their issue from a chance of succession. Brothers were also, in theory, refused succession rights, which helped to reduce the number of candidates intriguing for the throne. Succession disputes did occur in Dahomean history, but were infrequent by comparison with many other African races. Dahomey grew

67

stronger and stronger, until it became a child of its own military power.

* * *

Bullfinch Lamb gives one the feeling that the Kings of Dahomey were little worse than kindly eccentrics. Forty-eight years later there had been a change, described by Robert Norris in his book, *Memoirs of the Reign of Bossa Ahadee, King of Dahomey*. Norris, a trader, had hardly landed in Whydah when he came upon a tragedy which underlined that change. He visited the market and found the viceroy passing sentence of death on a middle-aged woman, who was on her knees before him. 'I requested her life might be spared', he wrote, 'but I was disappointed: He told me the king himself had considered the offence, and decreed the sentence; which was "that her head should be cut off, and fixed upon a stake" which was lying by her, and which she had been compelled to bring with her from Abomey for that purpose.

'During this conversation a little girl prompted by curiosity, and ignorant of what was doing, made her way through the crowd; and, discovering her mother, ran to her mother to congratulate her on her return (from Abomey). The poor woman, after a short embrace, said, "Go away, child, this is no place for you", and she was immediately conveyed away. The viceroy proceeded in his sentence, which the poor wretch heard with seeming indifference, picking her teeth with a straw which she took up from the ground. When the viceroy concluded his charge to the spectators, of obedience, submission, and orderly behaviour, which the king required from all his people, the delinquent received a blow on the back of her head, with a bludgeon, from one of the executioners which levelled her to the ground; and another severed it from her body with a cutlass. The head was then fixed on a pole in the market place, and the body was immediately carried to the outside of the town and left there to be devoured by wild beasts.' Her crime had been that of accidentally setting fire to a neighbour's hut.

Norris was to see many such sights in Abomey at the time of the Annual Customs but retained a cool enough head to report in detail on whatever he saw. Not long after he arrived there, he was sent for by the King. He unpacked his presents, 'a handsome sedan chair and a chamber organ' and went off to the palace gate. 'On each side of it was a human head, recently cut off, lying on a flat stone with the face down, the bloody end of the neck towards the entrance. In the guard-house were about forty women (these were some of the famous Amazon brigade who guarded the King) armed with a musket and cutlass each; and twenty eunuchs, with bright iron rods in their hands.' Norris was led through two courtyards where more severed heads were on display. He then passed through a third door and found the King seated 'on a handsome chair of crimson velvet, ornamented with gold fringe, placed on a carpet, in a spacious cool piazza, which occupied one side of the court. He was smoking tobacco, and had on a gold-laced hat, with a plume of ostrich feathers; he wore a crimson damask robe, wrapped loosely around him; yellow slippers and no stockings: several women were employed fanning him, and others with whisks to chase away the flies: one woman, on her knees before him, held a gold cup, for him to spit in.'

Norris presented the King with his gifts. The King appeared to be delighted with both, especially the sedan chair, and he spent a happy hour being carried round and round the court. Almost as an afterthought, Norris added: 'In the evening I purchased thirty-two slaves, which finished the business of the day.'

Norris, who was in Abomey in the early months of the year, experienced another of the country's unique aspects, the strange wind that blows from the north-east called the *harmattan*. He wrote: 'It comes on indiscriminately at any hour of the day or night; at any time of the tide, or at any period of the moon's age; and continues a day or two; sometimes five or six; once I knew it to continue a fortnight; and there are generally three or four returns of it every season.

'The wind is always accompanied with an unusual gloominess and haziness of the atmosphere; very few stars can be seen through the fog; and the sun, concealed the greatest part of the day, appears only for a few hours about noon, and then of a mild red, exciting no painful sensation in the eye. No dew is perceived during the continuance of this wind; nor is there the least appearance of any moisture in the atmosphere. Salt of

Tartar, dissolved in water, so as to run upon a tile, and exposed to the *harmattan*, even in the night, becomes perfectly dry again in a few hours. Vegetables of every kind suffer considerably from it: all tender plants, and seeds just sprouting above the earth are killed by it: the most flourishing evergreens feel its baneful influence; the branches of the lemon, orange and lime trees droop; the leaves become flaccid, and wither ... the grass withers and dries like hay. The covers of books, shut up closely in a trunk, and protected by lying among clothes, bend back as if they had been exposed to fire: the panels of doors, window shutters, etc, split; and the joints of a well-laid floor of seasoned wood, will gape so wide that one may lay his finger in them: the sides and decks of ships, become quite open and leaky and veneered work flies to pieces from the contraction of the wood in different directions.' Norris found that the air temperature dropped by as much as ten or twelve degrees when the wind sprang up and that if it blew for several days at a time he suffered, like the Dahomeans, from chapped lips and nostrils; if it blew for more than five days, large areas of skin sloughed away. But, like many other winds, this was alleged to have medical benefits: it was supposed to cure sores and cuts, help the fever-stricken, stop epidemics like small-pox, and ameliorate the flux. In April the rains began and the *harmattan* ceased to blow. It was during the *harmattan* season that most travellers journeyed to Abomey. It was also during that season that the King of Dahomey often honoured his ancestors with the Annual Customs which were to become so widely known. Norris was a witness to them, so was Burton.

4

BY THE beginning of 1864 West African slavery was in the last stages of decay, except in Dahomey. The trade's decline had been brought about by many factors, not the least of which was a more humanitarian spirit in the world. But there were more particular reasons, like the presence of the West African Squadron and the fact that American ships would no longer participate in slave transport.

Slavery itself had been changing in the past thirty years and

Bound and gagged, victims of the 'King's Head Thing', are brought into the royal presence before being executed.

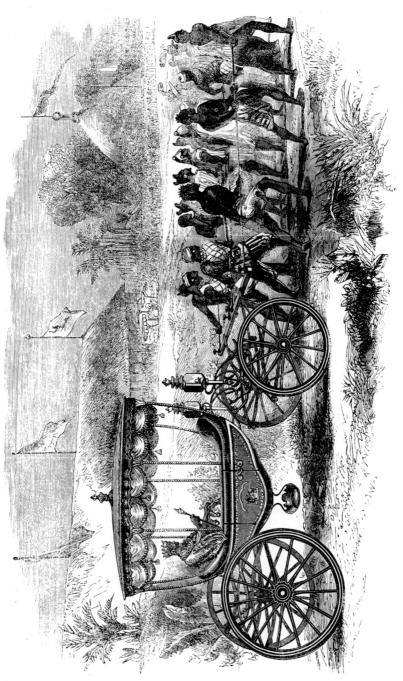

The King of Dahomey being drawn to a state ceremony in a carriage he received as a gift from Europe.

A Dahomean victim after execution is hung upside down outside the palace.

Dahomean Amazons. They were often used as shock troops in the wars with neighbouring states.

Richard Burton as he was when
he made his famous visit to
Dahomey.

The Royal Navy gunboat *Teaser* captures a slaver off the African coast in 1857.
More than **230** slaves were found in its stifling hold which measured
50 ft. × **20 ft.** × **3 ft. 6 in.**

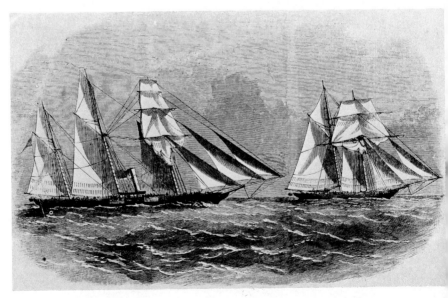

the days had long since gone when vessels could arrive on the African coast, fill up with slaves, and ply their peaceful passage back to America or Brazil. Britain abolished slavery in 1808 and from 1817 various countries, including Spain, Portugal, the Netherlands, Sweden and France granted her the right to stop and search their ships for slaves. But because America was not a signatory to the agreement—instead she sent a small squadron of her own to police American shipping—Britain's task became highly complicated. The case of the *Illinois* illustrates this: In 1843 the *Illinois* was discovered at the Dahomean slave port of Whydah by a British cruiser. The Royal Navy boarded her and discovered that she had American papers, which meant she could not be seized. She took aboard 430 slaves and set sail. She encountered the same British cruiser, which was lying off shore. But the captain of the *Illinois* thought the British cruiser had sailed off down the coast and that the vessel sighted was an American frigate. Immediately, he hoisted the Spanish flag. Spain had been a signatory to the British agreement so the British cruiser set off in pursuit. The *Illinois* saw her mistake, hauled down the Spanish flag and raised the American. Once again the British cruiser was helpless.

This sort of thing went on for some years and it became common for the captain of a slaver to 'sell' his vessel to a member of the crew whose nationality precluded the vessel from being searched since his government had signed no agreement. Finally it reached a point where something had to give. It did so in 1845 with the case of HMS *Wasp*. The *Wasp* had captured two Brazilian slavers, the *Felicidade* and the *Echo* off the coast of Africa and had put prize crews aboard. The *Echo* was carrying four hundred slaves and, while the *Felicidade* was empty, she was fully equipped for the trade. The prize crew on the *Felicidade* consisted of Midshipman Palmer and nine seamen. They were attacked by the Brazilians and knifed to death. The ship then hoisted her colours and sailed to the Slave Coast. There she was stopped and boarded by HMS *Star*. The boarding party found bloodstains and a Negro servant told them what had happened. Ten of the Brazilians were implicated in the murder and taken to Britain for trial.

71

The court ruled that since the *Felicidade* had no slaves on board and since Brazil had not signed a clause covering equipment, the original capture of the vessel had been illegal. The defendants were acquitted and sent back to Brazil.

As a result of the *Wasp* case, the attitude of British seamen on the Slave Coast hardened. Officers led boarding crews with the watchword, 'Remember the *Felicidade*!' There was no mercy for those who resisted. The crews of slavers were now often marooned on the coast to die of fever or by African spears, instead of being taken to Sierra Leone for trial.

At the end of the 1840s, Brazil, in spite of signing treaties outlawing the trade, was still the richest transatlantic market for slaves, taking fifty and sixty thousand a year. Britain lost patience and in 1849 despatched a squadron under Admiral Reynolds with orders to break up the Brazilian trade. Reynolds sailed into the harbour of Rio de Janeiro and burnt three slavers at their moorings. He then sailed along the coast seeking out slavers in every river and creek and destroying what he found. Brazilians were outraged. But their Foreign Minister, Paulino, could only reply, 'When a powerful nation like Britain is evidently in earnest, what can Brazil do?'

This sort of harassment eventually began to pay dividends in terms of West Africa. Those slavers who wanted to continue the trade began to search for ports in the Indian Ocean. The African states on the west coast—except for Dahomey—began to capitulate to pressure and, in some cases, more than pressure, for the abolition of slaving was used as an excuse by the great powers to colonize large sections of Africa. This meant that the West African Squadron could now give all its attention to Whydah.

5

I N THE 1860s Lagos was annexed by Britain and the presence of English missionaries in Abeokuta, where they were in constant danger from Dahomean attacks, added a political incentive for the British Government to bring pressure to bear on Dahomey. Invasion was discussed and, naturally, supported by Burton, but the Admiralty held back, unwilling to add to its responsibilities on the west coast. The only alternative was a diplomatic mission. In 1862 Commander Eardley-Wilmot, Officer Commanding the Squadron, went to Abomey to feel out King Gelele on an anti-slavery treaty. He seems to have been rather taken in by the King, for he left—*he* also promised to return but never did— naïvely confident that conditions were favourable for negotiation. When his naval duties kept him elsewhere, Burton was chosen for the return visit.

He received his orders in a letter from Lord Russell, the Foreign Secretary. After telling him to make certain that a proper reception was accorded him in Abomey, Russell went on: 'You will, on your arrival, inform the King, that the many important duties which devolve on Commodore Wilmot . . . have prevented him returning in person to confirm the good understanding which it is hoped has been established between the King and Her Majesty's Government by the Commodore's late visit . . .

'With regard to the question of the export of slaves from his territories, you will not fail to impress upon the King the importance which Her Majesty's Government attach to the cessation of this traffic.

'Her Majesty's Government admit the difficulties which the King may find in putting a stop to a trade that has so long existed in his country and from which his ancestors have derived so much profit, but his income from this source must be very small compared with that of former kings, and it will be to his interest to find out some other form of revenue, before that which he now derives from the sale of his fellow men to the slave-dealers is entirely put a stop to. You will remind the King that he himself suggested to Commodore Wilmot that if we wished to put a stop to the Slave trade, we should prevent white men from coming to buy them, and you will state that Her Majesty's Government have concluded a treaty with the United States Government which will prevent, for the future, any American vessels from coming to ship slaves.

'With regard to human sacrifice, I rejoice to find from Commodore Wilmot's report, that the number of victims at the King's Customs has been exaggerated.

'It is feared, however, that much difficulty will be

experienced in prevailing upon the King to put a stop to this barbarous practice, which prevails more or less openly along the greater part of the Western African coast.'

According to Russell, King Gelele had told Wilmot he would welcome English traders at Whydah and would help to rebuild the English fort there which had fallen into decay. Burton was to point out to Gelele that there should be a 'sufficiency of lawful trade to induce them to do so'. Russell continued: 'English merchants cannot take slaves in return for their goods, they must have oil, ivory, cotton, and such other articles as the country is capable of producing. The King will see, therefore, that it must depend very much on his own exertions, and those of his subjects, whether it will be worthwhile for British merchants to settle at Whydah.'

He pointed out that the presents for the King were those Gelele himself had asked Wilmot to get for him 'with the exception of the carriage and horses, and with respect to these you will explain to the King, that in the first place it would be a difficult matter to get English horses out to the Coast, and even supposing they arrive safely at their destination, it would be very doubtful from the nature of the country and climate, whether they would long survive their arrival.

'If, however, the future relations with the King should be of a nature to warrant such a proceeding, Her Majesty's Government would not hesitate to comply with his wishes, by sending him an English carriage and horses.'

The presents which Burton was to take with him comprised: 'One forty feet circular crimson silk Damask Tent with pole complete (contained in two boxes). One richly-embossed silver Pipe with amber mouthpiece in morocco case. Two richly embossed silver Belts with Lion and Crane in raised relief, in morocco cases. Two silver and partly gilt Waiters. One coat of Mail and Gauntlets.' One wonders what either the King, or the Foreign Secretary, had in mind for the Mail and Gauntlets. At most times of the year they would have induced heat-stroke. Perhaps sometime someone might consider a monograph on the diversity and number of useless presents sent to Africa by European governments in the eighteenth and nineteenth centuries. High on the list must come the mail and gauntlets as well as Norris's chamber organ which would have been wrenched out of tune the moment the *harmattan* began to blow. The Foreign Office must have had a long-lasting musical tradition for in the mid-nineteenth century we find a British consul carrying a box organ all the way from London to Abyssinia for the Emperor—who was incensed at the absurdity of the gift and gave it to a missionary.

Much of Burton's previous wandering had been done either incognito or as a private citizen. Now he was to travel in style. On November 29, 1863, he boarded the *Antelope* and sailed to the echoes of a seventeen-gun salute, landing at Whydah a few days later, where he spent five days. He found the town 'not exceedingly unhealthy, despite its extreme filth', but complained that there was no society left. 'The old days of sporting, picnics and processions, of dancing, loving, drinking and playing, are gone, probably never to return,' he wrote. 'The place is temporarily ruined and as dull as dull can be, except when the occasional breaking of the blockade gives a kind of galvanic life.' Two months before, a steamer had reached the open sea with nine hundred slaves aboard. Those in Whydah with an interest in slaving had celebrated the occasion with a banquet and, according to Burton, 'even the non-slaving traders and others were there drinking pro-slavery toasts ... All here is now in transition state. Slave exporting is like gambling, a form of intense excitement which becomes a passion; it is said that after once shipping a man, one must try to ship another. And the natives of Whydah give the licit dealer scanty encouragement. Having lived so long without severer toil than kidnapping, they are too old to learn labour, they allow their houses to fall, their plantations to become bush, their streets to be half grown with rank grass, and their swamps to reek undrained.'

He visited the English fort—in fact, Burton was the kind of traveller who saw *everything* and one must picture him out early in the morning until late at night with note-book and sketch pad; he was a man with an enormous appetite for work.[1] He found the building almost falling down and in the compound

[1] In 1878 when Burton was in Trieste a journalist found him at work on eleven different projects; each had its own room.

a fetish figure 'throned amid a mass of filth—yet the people wonder that they suffer from smallpox and measles'. He described another fetish figure which he saw in the town as 'squat, crouched, as it were, before its own attributes, with arms longer than a gorilla's, huge feet and no legs to speak of. The head is of mud or wood, rising conically to an almost pointed poll; a dab of clay represents the nose, the mouth is a gash from ear to ear, and the eyes and teeth are of cowries, or painted ghastly white. Legba is of either sex, but rarely feminine. Of the latter I have seen a few ... the breasts project like the halves of a German sausage and the rest is to match.'

The picture that emerges of Whydah is that of a decrepit tropical town decaying in the heat and humidity, its alleys and roads choked with grass or mud, its houses built away from each other, some collapsing, some only made of mats, and over everything the brooding presence of carrion crows, vultures and marabou storks.

Fourteen years before Burton's visit Commander Frederick Forbes visited Dahomey on an anti-slaving mission and in his book *Dahomey and the Dahomans* he wrote of Whydah: 'The principal building is the cha-cha's (King's agent's) house, a large ill-built erection of no particular form, occupying one side of the principal square; and, as nothing can be cleanly in Africa, opposite, occupying a side of the square, is a corral for cattle, seldom cleaned except by the animalcula of the exuviae that decay breeds.'

Having applied for and received permission to travel to Abomey, Burton set off on December 13 at the beginning of the *harmattan* season. His party consisted of John Cruikshank, a naval surgeon, the Reverend Peter Bernasko, described as a 'native assistant missionary', his son Tom, who was eleven, and several interpreters, even though Burton had already begun a study of the language. Some idea of the size of the operation might be gained from the fact that this group was attended by fifty-nine porters, thirty hammock-men to carry them, and sundry cooks and flag carriers, making a caravan of ninety-nine people. When Commander Forbes took the same road in 1849 his smaller party still needed twenty-six hammock-men, and thirty-six porters, twenty of whom were women. And there were an additional five women whose only function was to carry Forbes's money: he had changed fifty dollars into cowries and was faced with the staggering prospect of having to take 100,000 shells wherever he went.

As Burton's safari wound on its way, royal messengers began to arrive from Abomey. Each carried a carved stick which served as his credentials. They inquired solicitously after Burton's health and stayed to drink a glass of rum, of which he had a large supply.

The principal members of his party adopted the local form of transport, the hammock. Burton found it a 'not unpleasant conveyance, especially when the warmed back is a time cooled by walking. These barbarians, however, have not, like the Hindoos, invented a regular four-in-hand; two men are easily tired, especially by standing still, which is wearisome to them as to loaded camels. When they reach a rough place another pair, diving in between the usual number, roughly clutch the cloth at the rider's shoulders and heels, bumping, if possible, his pate against the pole.'

On the journey he met four of the famous 'Amazons', the Household Brigade of Abomey, whose duties were to guard the King, often to sleep with him, and in war to be used as an assault force. On Burton's secret visit to Dahomey he had been made a sort of Honorary Colonel-in-Chief of one of the Amazon troops; notwithstanding that, he did not care for them. 'The four soldieresses were armed with muskets, and habited in tunics and white colottes,' he wrote, 'with two blue patches meant for crocodiles (insignia). They were commanded by an old woman in a man's straw hat, a green waistcoat, a white shirt . . . a blue waistcloth, and a sash of white calico. Two of the women . . . were of abnormal size, nearly six feet tall, and of proportional breadth.' Contrasting the Amazons with the men, whom he found rather effeminate, he said, 'Such, on the other hand, was the size of the female skeleton, and the muscular development of the frame, that in many cases femininity could be detected only by the bosom.'

The idea of a tribe of ferocious fighting women has fascinated the world for thousands of years, and the word 'amazon' (lit. 'breastless') dates from ancient Greece. It was first used to describe a legendary race of female warriors said to have come from beyond the Caucasus and to have settled in Asia Minor.

77

They were governed by a queen, and according to some authorities the female children had their right breasts cut off in order to facilitate their use of the bow. Once a year the tribe cohabited with men of a different race and the resulting female children were trained in war; the male children were destroyed. Amazons frequently recur in Greek literature from Homer onwards and were believed to have invaded Attica in 1256 B.C.

The Dahomean Amazons certainly did not have their breasts cut off but in some other respects seem to conform to their legendary precursors. They were formed by King Agaja in about 1727 from a group of female elephant hunters. In his *History of Dahomy* published in 1793, Archibald Dalzel describes how Agaja 'armed a great number of women like soldiers, having their proper officers, and furnished like regular troops with drums, colours, and umbrellas, making at a distance a very formidable appearance.' With these shock troops he attacked and defeated a combined army made up of soldiers from Whydah and Popo.

To the Dahomean people the Amazons were known as 'mothers' and held the centre position, the most honoured, in battle. Forbes described the result of rivalry between the Amazons and the male soldiers: 'The amazons are not supposed to marry, and by their own statement, they have changed their sex. "We are men," say they, "not women." All dress alike, diet alike and male and female emulate each other: what the males do the amazons will endeavour to surpass. They all take great care of their arms (these were usually long-barrelled Danish muskets) polish the barrels, and, except when on duty, keep them in covers.' Forbes visited Abomey during the reign of King Gezo, Gelele's father, who, according to Burton 'ordered every Dahoman of note in the Kingdom to present his daughters, of whom the most promising were chosen, and he kept the corps clear of the servile and the captive. Gelele, his son, causes every girl to be brought to him before marriage, and, if she pleases, he retains her in the palace ... these girls, being royal wives, cannot be touched without danger of death ...'

Although the Amazons were supposed to remain celibate, Burton was soon to come across a large number who were pregnant and suggests that only about two-thirds of the women were virgins. Forbes ascribed their ferocity to their way of life. 'The extreme exercise of one passion,' he wrote, 'will generally obliterate the very sense of the others; the Amazons, whilst indulging in the excitement of the most fearful cruelties, forget the other desires of our fallen nature.' Burton demurred. All passions are sisters, he said and went on: 'I believe that bloodshed causes these women to remember, not to forget LOVE . . .' He saw troops of Amazons marching and said they were 'remarkable for a stupendous stratopyga, and for a development of adipose tissue which suggested anything but ancient virginity—man does not readily believe in fat "old maids".'

He described the Amazons as 'an evil' in the Dahomean empire. Wherever he went he remarked on the sparseness of the population and blamed much of this on the Amazons as an institution. 'The women troops, assumed to number 2,500, should represent 7,500 children; the waste of reproduction, and the necessary casualties of "service", in a region so de-populated, are as detrimental to the body politic as a propor-tional loss of blood would be to the frame personal. Thus the land is a desert, and the raw material of all industry, man, is everywhere wanting.'

On the march to Abomey he was also to encounter a facet of Dahomean life which irritated almost every traveller: whenever either the King's wives or the Amazon's slavewomen walked abroad no man was allowed to look at them. Their presence was heralded by a bell. J. A. Skertchly, the English zoologist who visited Abomey eight years after Burton and who was kept there by Gelele, a virtual prisoner, for nearly nine months, was rudely dumped by his hammock-men who fled into the tall grass at the side of the track when the bell was heard. Skertchly watched as five women filed past with water jars on their heads. The leading woman had a bell round her neck. He said: 'No man is permitted to meet them, while, if the tinkle of the bell is unheeded, they will stop and rattle it in high dudgeon until the baneful male scampers into the bush.

'This institution is one of the greatest nuisances in the country, for in the capital there are so many of these bands journeying from one of the royal palaces to another, that a

79

straightforward progress of twenty yards is scarcely practicable.' Clearly Burton found this onerous too and often did not give way, especially when out shooting in the early morning. He recounted how the women said, 'He is a white and knows no better.' At other times he would take out pencil and paper and pretend to sketch them. This caused them to flee.

<h1 style="text-align:center">6</h1>

KING GELELE met Burton in the town of Kana which lay just outside Abomey and was the site of the King's country palace. Here Burton experienced something that was to weary him throughout his stay: the need to dress up in his best uniform and wait in the sun, sometimes for hours, for the appearance of the King; the 'penance of reception', he called it. Skertchly's experience of the formality was so formidable that he broke into italics at the memory; Burton took a loftier tone. He was sent for at 10 a.m., but said he knew from experience that such ceremonies never took place until the afternoon so did not make an appearance until 1 p.m. when he and his party were shown a programme of dancing and singing. They had no sooner taken their seats than an old card table arrived—a present from Commander Wilmot to Gelele—on which were set bottles of rum, gin and wine. Burton had earlier decided to try and avoid the rough spirits in favour of Muscadel, but found this difficult in the face of repeated messages sent by the King urging him to drink up. At 2 p.m., to the sound of an occasional cannon shot, they were led to the palace and were allowed to enter once they had removed their ceremonial swords and closed their umbrellas, neither object being allowed to appear before the King. They were then guided through a courtyard and found King Gelele sitting in the shade on an 'earthbench' covered in red, blue and striped cotton cloths. Burton described him as being between forty and forty-five, tall and with an athletic body, broad-shouldered, muscular, with well-turned wrists, neat ankles, 'but a distinctly cucumber-shaped shin'. The face was jowly but strong and though his expression was hard, Burton found it open and not at all bad tempered. He wore his finger nails very long and Burton suggested that

African kings must show the talons of meat eaters to make it plain they do not live on 'monkey-food'—fruits and vegetables. His teeth were strong and white but some of the surfaces were covered with tobacco tar. His eyes were red and inflamed and Burton put this down to a variety of things: the glare, the wind, too much fornication; but mostly he blamed smoking; the King apparently smoked continuously.

The pipe was an institution in Dahomey. Norris remarked on it during his visit. Clay pipes from Europe were much in vogue and there was also a minor pipe-making industry in Abomey. The King's pipe was highly decorated and chased with silver and was put away in a special case when not needed. Burton says his tobacco pouch was 'nearly the size of a modern carpet bag. The Dahomeans, even the King, use Brazilian roll and American leaf; a few prefer the worst kind of cigars.'

Gelele's face was pitted by small-pox scars and his skin was not so much black as reddish-brown; there were rumours that his mother was a mulatto from the Whydah. His dress on this occasion was simple, a plain white cotton body-cloth edged with watered green silk, drawers of purple flowered silk reaching to mid-thigh and Moorish sandals embroidered in gold. For jewellery he wore bracelets, an armband, a single blue bead and a fetish charm in the shape of a human incisor that hung round his neck and was supposed to ward off illness.

At this first meeting Burton began to get some idea of the veneration in which the Dahomeans held their kings. Gelele was looked upon as a god, his word was final, his power absolute. This had its snags since the power and divinity overshadowed the man, which meant that it was almost impossible for Gelele to institute changes—in the Annual Customs, for instance—without weakening his own position.

He was surrounded by wives and Amazons. Through open doorways Burton could see slave girls peering out at him. None appealed to him physically, but they atoned for their homeliness by their extreme devotion to the King. 'If perspiration appears upon the royal brow it is instantly removed with the softest cloth by the gentlest hands; if the royal dress be disarranged it is at once adjusted; if the royal lips move, a plated spittoon, which, when Mr Norris wrote, was gold, held by one of the wives, is moved within convenient distance; if the King sneezes, all present touch the ground with their foreheads; if he drinks, every lip utters an exclamation of blessing.'

After grasping Burton's hand and 'snapping fingers' the King inquired after the health of Queen Victoria, the state of the Foreign Office and of the British people and when Burton had reassured him on all three points they sat down in an atmosphere of great goodwill. Gelele could not get over the fact that Burton had returned as promised and remarked on this more than once. As they raised their glasses to toast Queen Victoria the visitors received a shock. The King suddenly wheeled round and two of his wives raised a screen of white calico between him and the others so that no one might see him drink. Each time there was a toast—and there were several, including one to Burton—the same ritual was observed, and each time there was a prodigious outburst of noise: guns were fired, Amazons rang their bells and high officials bent to the ground clapping their palms. When the toasts were done, salutes were fired, the first for royalty, then eleven guns for Commander Wilmot and nine for Burton. This did not suit him at all and he demanded the same number as his predecessor. Despite the fact that his interpreter 'turned blue' with apprehension Burton insisted he tell the King, who quickly apologized and ordered two more guns fired. Honour satisfied, the visitors left the presence.

It was during this time that Burton saw several decorated skulls said to have been those of the most important chiefs Gelele had killed. He was surprised at how well kept they were. This was part of Dahomean tradition. Norris was told by King Adahoonzou II that if he, the King, fell into the hands of his enemies he wished to be treated 'with that decency of which I set the example'. Burton noted that one of the skulls was that of Akia'on, chief of Attako near Porto Novo, who was taken by Gelele three years before. 'Beautifully white and polished, it is mounted in a ship or galley of thin brass about a foot long, with two masts, and jib-boom, rattlings, anchor, and four portholes on each side . . . when King Gezo died his successor (Gelele) received a message from this chief, that all men were now joyful, that the sea had dried up, and that the world had seen the bottom of Dahome. Gelele rejoined by slaying him, and mounting his skull in a ship, meaning that there is still water enough to float the kingdom, and that if the father is dead the son is still alive.'

Burton also saw the ritual observed by even the most important people of the land when they came to greet the King: they rubbed themselves on the ground and threw handfuls of dust on their arms and shoulders. This offended him as it had done Forbes, who described the ritual compliments Dahomeans paid the King as 'filthy praise'.

On December 20, Burton entered Abomey. The King and his suite followed the next day. Gelele was detained at Kana because 150 of his Amazons were found to be pregnant: 'So difficult is chastity in the Tropics,' wrote Burton. Several of the women were sentenced to death with their lovers, the men being saved up to die at the Customs, the Amazons to be executed in the privacy of the palace which Burton found 'more civilized than Great Britain, where they still, wondrous to relate, "hang away" even women, and in public.'

* * *

Abomey, rainbow's end for a traveller from the coast, was no great hidden city of grandeur and wealth, but a big rambling place of mud houses built behind mud walls, parts of which were crumbling. Dalzel described the central area as 'an assemblage of farmyards with long thatched barns', from which Burton did not dissent. Forbes wrote, 'The city is about eight miles in circumference, surrounded by a ditch about five feet deep, filled with prickly acacia, its only defence. It is entered by six gates, which are simply clay walls crossing the road, with two apertures, one reserved for the King, the other a thoroughfare for his subjects. In each aperture are two human skulls . . .' Inside the city walls was a great deal of wasteland as well as many cultivated small-holdings. It was an easy place to get lost in. There were no regular streets and all the houses were surrounded by high red clay walls which also enclosed banana and orange trees. Water was a problem. The nearest supply was five miles away and every drop had to be brought in by hand.

Skulls and the larger human bones still ocupied places on the walls when Burton entered the city. He also noted skulls hanging from several doors as he passed. He was taken to a hut which was to be his lodging and described it as a barn forty-five feet long and twenty-seven feet wide, roofed with heavy thatch that came down to within five feet of the ground. The rooms were dark and close and he had a hole knocked through the wall of one to let in more air. He made a shutter for the opening from a claret case and turned the place into a 'tolerable study'.

The next day he visited the main palace. He travelled by hammock and on the way there saw a man standing, gagged, in front of a drummer. Burton was told that he was a criminal awaiting execution at the forthcoming Customs. The gag was a ferocious instrument, a Y–shaped stick, the sharp end of which was wedged against the palate while the fork held down the tongue. The gag was used in case the man managed to speak to the King when, according to Dahomean custom, he would have to be pardoned.

At the palace Burton's party was kept waiting for three hours for the ceremony which would mark the arrival of Gelele. But the old card table was set up before them and Burton passed the time sampling the liquors—he tried to stick to the Muscadel but boredom and frustration gave him a harder head and he drank the trade gin and the rum as well as some liquor he had brought along himself. He was gradually joined by other *caboceers* (dignitaries or headmen) such as Buko-no, a fetish man who owned the house in which he was staying, and Prince Chyudaton, a Dahomean aristocrat, who arrived 'riding a little nag, as if on side saddle, and shaded by an umbrella hat of worn palm leaves'. The prince was sucking a lettuce leaf. For further entertainment an Abeokutan prisoner-of-war danced for them and Burton made the point that not all such captives were killed or sold. In mid-afternoon the King arrived at last. A long line of flags and umbrellas— multi-coloured parasols and umbrellas were *de rigueur* in Abomey—were seen coming in the gates of the palace. With thudding drums and the firing of muskets the procession paraded around the courtyard. There were thirty-three different groups of *caboceers*, royal relatives, fetish men and

84

other important folk. Last of all came King Gelele with five hundred musketeers, a skull standard, bobbing umbrellas, swaying flags, drums, rattles and horns. The king himself rode in a carriage pulled by men and was shaded by four white umbrellas. Behind him came a crowd of slaves carrying chairs, boxes, baskets and cowrie shells, bottles and other valuables. In the midst of the din and dust, Gelele was carried ten times round the courtyard in a bath-chair—a present from England —while he covered his mouth to keep out the dust. Burton noted that he looked weary and cross, 'an expression not unfrequent upon the brow of royalty in all lands'. The male soldiers retired and the Amazons gave a display of dancing and singing to the *obbligato* of musket fire. They were accompanied not only by the usual coloured umbrellas and flags but also by platters of skulls, women carrying weapons like long cut-throat razors, rattles, cymbals and drums. Twelve of the women then proceeded to carry the King round the yard in a hammock of yellow silk.

The colourful ceremony was punctuated every now and then by presents of more liquor from Gelele. Perhaps it was the drink, perhaps the riotous display, perhaps both: in the event, Burton retired 'with the usual finale to a Dahomean parade—a headache'.

The following day he presented the official gifts to the King, and made the mistake of giving him not only those sent by the Foreign Office but also the gifts he had brought himself. He assumed that his munificence might result in his being able to deliver his message from the British Government at the very start of the visit so that he would be able to leave Abomey at any time he wished thereafter. Had he kept back some of the gifts he might have been able to bargain for an audience. But subtlety in dealing with people in powerful positions had never been one of Burton's points. He regarded the gift ceremony as a trial, so the sooner it was over the better. And this turned out to be so. The main present, the 'forty feet circular crimson silk Damask Tent with pole complete . . .' was found to be too small. Burton and his party were obliged to pitch it themselves and found it complicated. The tent pegs were made of wood and, of course, would not have lasted long in a land where white ants are endemic. It was apparently quite pretty when they finally got it up (more so than anything belonging to the King, Burton thought), yet the only part of it admired was the gingerbread lion on the pole-top. Of the other presents: the pipe was never used because Gelele liked his old one better; the belts caused disappointment because apparently Commander Wilmot had been asked, not for belts, but for bracelets; the silver waiters were much admired but no one knew what they were for; the gauntlets were too small and the coat of mail was too heavy. Burton imagined it would be hung up and used for target practice, but he was wrong. It was still there when Skertchly visited Abomey. Gelele showed it to him and then made one of his wives put it on, commenting that the English must be very strong to fight encumbered by such a weight. It was clear that apart from the waiters the presents had been a disappointment. The King constantly pressed for the horses and carriage. 'I vainly, for the dozenth time, explained the difficulty of sending them. It was disposed of at once with consummate coolness. Carriages had been brought, and could come again. If the horses died upon the beach at Whydah, no matter. King Gezo, after obtaining an equipage, had taken the strong name Nun-u-pwe-to, and the son burned to emulate the sire.' Clearly annoyed at the reception of the presents Burton, in the voluminous daily diary of his mission, had some scathing suggestions for gifts that *would* be appreciated: '. . . children's toys, gutta-percha faces, Noah's Arks; in fact, what would be most acceptable to a child of eight—which the Negro is.'

The King remained silent throughout the presentation. But 'his disappointment soon pierced through his politeness, which was barely retained by a state of feeling best expressed by our popular adage, "Better luck next time," especially in the matter of an English carriage and horses'. Burton then asked whether he could deliver his message but was told that he would have to await another opportunity. He was dismissed with a decanter of rum and a bottle of Médoc, which had gone sour.

7

TO THOSE emissaries like Forbes and Burton who came with the express purpose of delivering a message from Her Majesty's Government, the time spent at Abomey awaiting the King's pleasure must have seemed frustrating. But if Gezo and Gelele had seen them on their arrival and sent them off the following day we would have been denied many facts about the life of the Dahomeans in Abomey.

Skertchly has inveighed against Gelele for keeping him at Abomey for so long, but his book is a record of that period. It not only demonstrates his prejudices but also confirms many things that Burton had written. Skertchly was on less certain ground when he wrote in *Dahomey As It Is* of things of which he had no experience like 'buffalo-eating pythons', which he described as 'occasionally to be met with on the plains'. He passed some of his time by pretending to doctor the locals. A man was brought to him whose arm had been shattered by a bursting musket. Skertchly refused to help him. He saw that the man was seriously injured and tried to excuse his callousness by saying that if the man had died he would have been accused of killing him. Dwarfs, hunchbacks, palsied old people, men with withered arms, the blind, the deaf, the dumb and the lame, all came to Skertchly for help. He related with amusement how he gave them a mixture of curry powder, carbolic acid and camphor.

Burton was a different person entirely. Although he affected irritation, boredom and a generally patronizing attitude, he was a scholar and spent his life in search of facts, even if he sometimes got them wrong. For instance, he only spent two months in Dahomey yet he pried the secrets of Afa divination from Buko-no; learned the complex organization of the Dahomean government; studied the funeral, marriage and religious customs of the people and learned all he could about human sacrifice and the Amazons. Most important of all, by the time he left he could carry on a conversation in the Fon language. He followed his usual practice of study, helped by his extraordinary memory (at one time he could recite a quarter of the Koran by heart). In languages with written grammars he would first buy a simple textbook and vocabulary and underline the words and rules he felt should be memorized. He carried these books with him everywhere and studied them whenever he had a spare moment during his working day. By this method he learned on average three hundred new words a week. When he had acquired a basic vocabulary, he chose a simple story book and read it, marking with a pencil any new words he wanted to remember. Then he went on to a more difficult book. When he came across a new sound not found in any other language he trained his tongue by repeating it hundreds of times a day. In the case of Fon, he probably made his own vocabulary and grammar through notes of his conversations, recording new words and phrases. His facility gave him a supreme advantage in communication over other travellers in Dahomey.

Until his book was published the world looked upon the country as a kind of charnel house. There were stories that the King walked to his throne along a pathway ankle-deep in human gore, that he paddled about in a canoe in a tank of human blood, that he sacrificed two thousand people in a single day. It is interesting to contrast these stories with the conclusion of the French historian E. F. Gautier who, in 1935, called the old Dahomean monarchy the most advanced form of political organization in the black world.

There is no doubt that a great deal of cruelty existed but there was much else besides. One of the main virtues of the people was their diligence. While numerous famines are recorded in the Niger region to the north there is scarcely any record of famine in Dahomey. According to the economic historian Karl Polanyi, it is this diligence that made a success of the Dahomean agricultural policy, a fact made more remarkable when one remembers the drain on manpower caused by constant warfare. A 'Minister of Agriculture', the Tokpo, had responsibility for administering the policy of the country. He and his officials decided where certain crops were to be grown, for instance, millet near Abomey, maize and manioc between Whydah and Allada. Conservation was practised from early times. The output of palm wine was safeguarded by the King's ruling that no palm wine could be made except from trees growing wild in the bush. A census was taken each year at the end of the rainy season. This was much more exhaustive than anything done today. A total count was taken of the population and of the numbers of cultivators, weavers, potters, hunters, blacksmiths, slaves, etc. Then the food stocks throughout the kingdom were measured; a check was made on the number of palm trees, cattle, sheep, poultry and manufactured goods. Taxes were assessed on the basis of these totals. The total population figure was a state secret, known only to the King, and any village or provincial chief who disclosed the figures for his group would have been killed.

There was taxation. Pig farmers, for instance, paid one pig a year. Cattle, sheep and goat farmers were taxed once every three years, when up to an eighth of their herds was taken. Only wealthy people owned horses. Each horse was rated at four thousand cowries annually. Every trade or craft was liable for taxation. Internal trade was also taxed. A 'passport' system was used to keep count of porters who carried goods through tollhouses and there was a tollhouse at the entrance to every town. There was also a tax on inheritance. Forbes said that everything was taxed and the tax went to the King. 'If a cock crows near the highway, it is forfeited to the tax gatherer and, consequently, on the whole distance from Abomey to Whydah, the cocks are muzzled.' He also commented on the severity of the law: treason, murder, adultery, cowardice and theft were punishable by death. Although the King was generous in his gifts of hard liquor to the whites who came to his court, drunkenness was frowned upon among the Dahomeans and the King kept his own drunkard. He fed him on rum, exhibiting him at the Customs so that his pitiful condition might serve as a warning. The King also had his own 'smoker', not this time to serve as an awful example but in fact the occupier of a much-favoured office. Burton described him as one of the true African fantasticals. He carried a long-stemmed pipe and was supplied from the King's pouch.

Prostitution existed and was controlled by the King. The prostitutes were known as 'public women' and were sent to live in various parts of the country. At first, payment for their services was twenty cowries, but inflation raised this fourfold. According to Dalzel the women were appointed as a precaution by the Government to prevent the peace of private families being violated, and this was perhaps more necessary in Dahomey than in any other state, as adultery was 'severely punished and every indiscretion of gallantry exposes the delinquents to death or slavery . . .' There was also the fact that many Dahomeans were required to abstain from sex while their wives suckled an infant—usually three years—because it might cause sickness in future children.

The centre of the Dahomean universe was the royal household: here State and King combined. For instance, the King's wives, estimated at two thousand, were expected to play their part in the administration of the State. Others were employed at various crafts. Some of the King's children acted as special messengers and performed other duties in the King's service. And although such people as ministers, tax collectors, auditors and the like lived in their own houses, they were supplied with food from the palace. The actual palace building was large. Each King built a gateway of his own which consisted of a gap in the wall closed by rough wooden doors. A long barnlike structure was erected near the gate and here the King, with his court around him, would dispense justice and perform his royal duties.

The most interesting aspect of Dahomey's governing tradition was its 'doubling' of people in key jobs. The administration was known for its honesty and reliability and Gautier rates its excellence beyond that of any other African state. One of the ways in which this came about was to create a female counterpart to every male official. This duality went right through the nation, even to the King.

The female doubles were called 'mothers' and within the palace the King had a complete counterpart of the administrative apparatus throughout the kingdom. It was the duty of each woman to know intimately all the administrative affairs of her male counterpart and keep a constant check on his operations. So whenever an official reported to the King on any matter, the *naye* (mother), his double, was there to give her version if it differed. Dualism also existed in the army, which was divided into a right and left wing. Each wing was split into a male regiment and a female regiment. Every male, from the highest-ranking officer down to the last soldier, had his female counterpart. The right wing was commanded by the *mingan*, the

Prime Minister, and his counterpart was the 'she-*mingan*' who, according to Burton, took precedence. Burton himself had a 'mother' in Abomey, who was assigned to him by the palace. This was the custom for all visitors to the capital and it was her duty to look after his needs during his stay; she was present at all audiences with the King.

Dualism found its strangest manifestation in the kingship: Gelele was two kings in one, the Town King and the Bush King. The Town King lived in the palace in Abomey; the Bush King, *Addo-Kpon*, had his palace at Kana. Each had its own complete establishment. Skertchly says the reason was that the office of kingship in Dahomey was so great that the King could never soil his hand by commercial dealings; but since the wealth of the country depended upon the sale of slaves and oil—the former being an exclusive royal monopoly, and the greater part of the oil exported from the country also from the King—how could these be sold without reducing the monarch to the position of a petty trader? 'There was the rub. Gezo surmounted this difficulty by the invention of the bush King, who could take all the onus of ignoble trade, leaving the true monarch to rule over his subjects and spend his revenues ... All the oil and palm kernels sold at Whydah are the produce of *Addo-Kpon*'s plantations, but Gelele buys the rum, powder and cloth; a very convenient way of getting a good name for spending money ...'

* * *

'At Benin ... they crucified a fellow in honour of my coming— here nothing! And this is the bloodstained Land of Dahome!!' Thus Burton in a letter to his friend Monckton Milnes. And, in what is described by his biographer Byron Farwell as 'in the same light vein', he had promised to send another friend, Fred Hankey, a human skin stripped from a living human victim, preferably a woman. This is typical Burton bravura, re- miniscent of the attitude which, when he was a small boy in France and had witnessed a guillotine execution, had led him to adapt the idea for a new game at school. Never squeamish about violence he had also, at Oxford, attempted to call out a fellow-student who had remarked derisively on his impressive moustaches. Luckily, the young man had had the wit to apologize. In Dahomey Burton had, in fact, sent a message to the court that he officially objected to being present at any human sacrifice and suggesting that animals be substituted. He threatened to leave at once, with or without permission, if any death took place in his presence. Having made his official position clear it seems reasonable to assume he would privately have been fascinated. However, though he was there for the period of the Customs, he saw no one actually killed.

For some days after the giving of the presents he was aware of growing nervousness and excitement in the Abomey air and *caboceers* began to arrive from outlying districts. He celebrated Christmas first in a hot rain, then in a *harmattan*. Three days later the Customs began.

Human sacrifice was not uncommon in West Africa among the tribes of the littoral and the forests, and according to some scholars it was not necessarily a matter of terror or dismay. Royal wives, relatives, and servants expected to die when the King himself died, how else would they gain honour among those on the other side? Those who were close to the King may simply not have wished to live without him. In some states human sacrifice grew in a reverse ratio to the decline of the slave trade.

Basil Davidson writes, 'What seems to have happened in some of the states that were profoundly affected by the coastal trade was that the custom of human sacrifice became increasingly distorted, both into a means of "conspicuous consumption" by display of wealth in slaves and, as time went on, into an instrument of political repression. Certainly the distortion grew worse. Its occasional terror reached a climax in the years of acute commercial insecurity that followed on the abolition of the slave trade. Then, with the mainstay of these societies cut suddenly away, superstition sank to gruesome depths . . . '

In the mid-seventeenth century Dapper was writing of Benin, 'No person of rank or wealth dies there unaccompanied by bloodshed.' But as a later writer pointed out, servants often begged to be allowed to die with their master, indeed in some cases only a favoured few, those best qualified to serve him, were despatched. But by the mid-nineteenth century the killings had accelerated in Benin into a kind of generalized mayhem. A European missionary has left an account of what occurred after the death of King Eyamba V at Old Calabar in 1847: 'Eyamba had many wives of the best families in the country, as also many slave concubines ... Of the former, thirty died the first day. How many by the poison ordeal, under imputation of witchcraft against his life, we never knew. Those who were honoured to accompany him into *Obio Ekpu*, or Ghost Land, were summoned in succession by the message, once an honour, now a terror, "King calls you". The doomed one quickly adorned herself, drank off a mug of rum, and followed the messenger. Immediately she was in the hands of the executioners, who strangled her with a silk handkerchief ...' The killings continued each evening, some victims were taken to the river and drowned, others beaten to death. After the holocaust the missionaries tried to get laws passed forbidding human sacrifice but it was not until a revolutionary secret society group called the Blood Men—whose object was to save, not shed blood—was formed that the massacres ended.

During Burton's visit the Annual Customs in Dahomey resulted in eighty deaths; all of the executed were either criminals or captive war prisoners. The Customs themselves formed a part of the very essence of monarchical rule. The King was looked upon as divine, the link between the people and the deified ancestors. He was also the guardian of the people's livelihood. The two functions came together at the Customs which was the principal event in the annual economic cycle and the time when some of the Kingdom's wealth was redistributed. During the Customs the King received gifts, payments and tributes; he then gave back part of them to the crowd. On the economic aspect, Polanyi wrote that it may be analysed as 'a move of goods and money towards the centre and out of it again, that is, redistribution. It was the main occasion of building up the finances of the royal administration and of distributing cowries among the people.' Its religious aspect was expressed by Melville J. Herskovits, who was one of the first to bring the complexity of Dahomey's culture to the attention of the world. Writing in the 1930s, he said: 'In the life of every Dahomean his ancestors stand between him and the gods ... the respect and worship of the ancestors may then be thought of as one of the great unifying forces that, for the Dahomean, give meaning and logic to life.'

Burton felt that the Customs had been thoroughly misunderstood in Europe. The King took no pleasure in the tortures and deaths, nor in the sight of blood. 'The two thousand killed in one day, the canoe paddled in a pool of gore, and other grisly nursery tales,' he put down to the romantic lies of slave-traders in Whydah who probably invented them to deter people from visiting the King. Whatever the reasons, he felt it was hypocritical to lay any blame on the Dahomeans when 'in the year of Grace 1864 we hung four murderers upon the same gibbet before 100,000 gaping souls at Liverpool, when we strung up five pirates in front of Newgate . . . and when our last Christian King but one killed a starving mother of seventeen with an infant at her breast, for lifting a yard of linen from a shop counter. A Dahomean visiting England but a few years ago would have witnessed customs almost quite as curious as those which raise our bile now.' Burton believed that the African victims were killed without cruelty: '. . . These negroes have not invented breaking on the wheel or tearing to pieces their victims . . .'

He thought Dahomey showed up rather well in comparison with Abeokuta, Ashanti and Benin. When he visited Benin in 1860 a sacrifice had just been performed. At Komasi a man was sacrificed every day except on Wednesdays which were the King's birthdays, and the death of any important person was followed by a minor blood-bath. By contrast, in Dahomey only a single slave was killed on the death of the Prime Minister or his 'double'. But so ingrained was human sacrifice he felt that to abolish it would mark the end of Dahomey itself. 'The practice originates from filial piety. It is sanctioned by long use and custom, and it is strenuously upheld by a powerful and interested priesthood. That, as our efforts to abolish the slave export trade are successful, these horrors will greatly increase, there is no room to doubt. Finally, the present king is for the present committed to them; he rose to power by the goodwill of the reactionary party and upon it he depends.'

There were two forms of Customs. The first was the Grand Customs, 'The King's Head Thing'. which took place on the death of a King. Burton, though he never witnessed a Grand

Customs—fortunately, perhaps, for it was a fearsome time—wrote: 'Human sacrifice in Dahomey is founded on a purely religious basis. It is a touching instance of the King's filial piety, deplorably mistaken, but perfectly sincere. The Dahoman sovereign . . . must enter Deadland with royal state, accompanied by a ghostly court . . .'

One of the earliest brief accounts of a Grand Customs comes from Dalzel, who ended his *History* thus: '1791. In the months of January, February and March, the solemnization of the Grand Customs, and of the King's Coronation, took place; the ceremonies of which lasted the whole three months, and were marked almost every day with human blood. Captain Fayrer, and particularly Mr Hogg, Governor of Apollonia, were present; and both affirm that not less than 500 men, women and children, fell as victims to revenge and ostentation, under the shew of piety: many more were expected to fall; but a sudden demand for slaves having thrown the lure of avarice before the King, he, like his ancestors, showed he was not insensible to its temptation.'

Of the Annual Customs, 'The Yearly Head Thing', Burton said they were first heard of in Europe in the days of King Agaja, in the early eighteenth century, though they had doubtless been practised many years before him. They were an extension of the Grand Customs and their function was to supply the departed monarch with fresh attendants in the shadowy world. For Burton, they began on December 28, 1863.

The day opened with a volley of muskets after which Burton received a message from the King saying that the Customs had begun and that they were expected at the Palace. About noon he went, with his party, to the market place and the first thing he saw was the victim shed. From a distance it looked like an English village church—a barn and tower. It was about one hundred feet long, forty feet wide and sixty feet high and it held twenty victims. Each man was sitting on a stool close to one of the supporting pillars to which he was tied in a complex series of loops, one of which passed round his neck. But Burton said the confinement was not cruel; each victim had an attendant next to him to keep off the flies, all were fed four times a day and at night they were untied and allowed to

95

sleep. They were dressed in the garb of state criminals, white shirts with scarlet trimmings and a blood-red heart sewn on to the left breast. On their heads they wore long white hats like dunces' caps. Burton felt that under similar restraint European prisoners would probably have tried to escape and probably have succeeded: 'These men will allow themselves to be led to slaughter like lambs.' He went on: 'I imagine it is the uncertainty of their fate that produces this remarkable *nonchalance*. They marked time to music and they chattered together especially remarking us. Possibly they were speculating on the chances of a pardon.'

Skertchly also noticed this seeming lack of worry when he attended the Annual Customs a decade later. He disagreed with Burton's theories, saying he had seen men laughing 'who knew their heads would be stuck at the palace gate within five minutes'. His thesis was that 'the dull brain of the negro is too sluggish to permit any future fate to influence his passions for good or evil'. Perhaps it was his enforced stay at Abomey which gave him such abrasive opinions of the blacks; whatever the reason, Burton sounded like a pink liberal by comparison.

The Customs at which Burton was to be a spectator were called the 'So-sin Customs' ('the house-tie thing') and took a total of five days to perform. They took their name from the fact that the Captain of the King's House, the *Sogan*, confiscated all houses from their wealthy owners, who were obliged to redeem them after a few days with bags of cowries.

Once again Burton and his party were seated in a good position to view the proceedings and they had not been sitting long when a cannon, fired inside the palace, announced that royalty was on its way. A corps of Amazons formed two lines outside the palace gate and down it stalked Gelele, accompanied by a group of his wives, on his way to perform a fetish ritual so that the proceedings could start. While he was doing this Burton noticed more victims in a second shed and his description is uncharacteristically compassionate. 'I counted nine victims on the ground floor and ten above . . . They resembled in all points those of the market shed, and looked wholly unconcerned, whilst their appearance did not attract the least attention. Yet I felt haunted by the presence of these

96

morituri, with whose hard fate the dance, the song, the dole (grief) and the noisy merriment of the thoughtless mob afforded the saddest contrast.' Near the victims sat the fetish men who stared at Burton and his party with a 'not over-friendly eye'. It is no great wonder, for wherever Burton went he ostentatiously used his notebook and sketch pad and these were regarded with the gravest suspicion. When the King finished his ritual, he and Burton snapped fingers and asked after each other's health and then the King went to lie on a couch strewn with cloths and shaded by umbrellas. Burton estimated there was a crowd of two thousand five hundred which included about three hundred children.

After some preliminary dancing, Gelele stepped forward to make a speech, the burden of which was that his father, Gezo, had improved the Annual Customs when he was King, as Gelele was trying to do in his turn. And he piously hoped that his children would do as much in his memory. At the end of his speech he retired behind a curtain to refresh himself, then reappeared to sing and dance for his people, at which he was assisted by two 'leopard wives', the youngest and prettiest of his harem who were dressed in white waistcoats and striped loin-cloths. Before sitting the King wiped the sweat from his forehead and, with a jerk, scattered it over the delighted group nearest him. Gelele finally settled down to listen to praises of himself before rising once more to reward publicly several captains in his army by promoting them to higher ranks. Later in the day he came over to the visiting party, which consisted of Burton, Dr Cruikshank and the Reverend Bernasko, and said he was expecting them to dance, sing and drum. Dr Cruikshank and Burton agreed to dance because they knew it was expected of them, but Gelele postponed this trial, saying that when he did call them he would make it in the cool of evening as the sun did not suit white men.

Late in the day Burton left, but not before he had sent a second message to Prince Chyudaton officially objecting to being present at any human sacrifice. He was reassured. In fact, there were no plans to execute any of the victims before the end of the So-sin Customs. In hindsight Burton dismissed the day's proceedings as poorer than those of any hill rajah in India. 'All was a barren barbarism, whose only "sensation" was produced by a score of men looking on and hearing that they were about to die.'

* * *

During the Customs, Burton wrote, ' . . . the labour of pleasure in Dahome is somewhat hard.' After the first day the Reverend Bernasko had to go to bed with 'a harmattan'. Burton does not explain what this mysterious ailment was and one is left with the impression of the good clergyman drying up and splitting like wood. They begged off and the King postponed the Customs for that day. On December 30 the Customs were revived and Burton and his party took their places in the afternoon. They had to wait two hours before the King made his appearance, but it was worth waiting for. He arrived wearing a skull cap of straw decorated with a brilliant striped cloth riding side-saddle on 'a little dingy nag'. Behind his lion-umbrella and parasol came a group of singing Amazons carrying seven skulls mounted on fancy flags. They were followed in turn by a dozen 'leopard wives' and a rearguard of old women and small girls.

The King mounted a platform and took off his clothes, keeping on a pair of shorts made of dark satin with yellow flowers. From his left shoulder hung a long sash of crimson silk and a short, silver-mounted sword. He put on a toga of a kind of green mosquito netting and took in his right hand what looked like a large bright billhook. He formed an effective figure against the glowing western sky. He then treated them to a series of dances, all in what Burton describes as the 'decapitation style'. After each dance he would rest and take some rum and occasionally would send some over to Burton. Once, indeed, sending over one of the brass-mounted skulls to be used as a drinking cup. By the end of the afternoon he had danced thirty-two times and began to give away decanters of rum which, Burton said, was a sure sign he was weary of pleasure.

The third day of the Customs was given over to the distribution of money to his people. The Dahomeans knew exactly what was to come and prepared for it. The King mounted his platform on which a great number of cowries had been placed;

his people, in Burton's words, 'removed their ornaments and girt their loins'. It was, apparently, tradition to fight for the royal largess. 'No notice is taken if a man be killed or maimed in the affair; he has fallen honourably fighting for his sovereign. Some lose eyes and noses . . . I have seen a hand through which teeth met . . . We speedily withdrew our chairs.' The King took strings of cowries and threw them high in the air. The bundles were torn to pieces in a moment, so were the strings, and some times a serious fight would break out over a single cowrie shell. The King, surrounded by his guard, then walked around the square, still throwing strings of cowries into the crowd and gradually a cloud of dust obscured almost everything, so great was the scramble and the fighting. The point of all this was that Dahomey knew no credit. In the markets payment for goods was by cash only. This form of annual distribution, eccentric as it might have appeared, did put money into circulation.

Later Burton himself was summoned by the King and he and his party had to scrabble like children in the dust as the King hurled strings of cowries at their feet. After a series of dances performed by hunchbacks Gelele walked to the victim-shed and slowly paced the length of it among the *morituri*. Every now and then he would throw two or three heads of cowries to one of the victims and these were gathered up and placed on their caps. He then joined Burton and gave him a hint that if he pleaded on behalf of the victims it was possible that some might be spared. Burton had been expecting this and co-operated, saying that mercy was the great prerogative of kings. This seemed to please Gelele for on his orders nearly half the prisoners were untied, brought before him and made to crouch on all fours to hear the royal lips utter the reprieve. He then gave Burton two decanters of rum, which meant that they had their 'pass' or permission to leave the presence.

The Customs continued their merry way with dancing, singing, parading, feasting and drinking, a good share of the latter partaken by Burton. But there was much more: it was a time when all great palavers were settled, when wrongdoers were punished and rewards were conferred on those who merited them. It was a time when the spoils of the previous war were divided up, when officers were promoted in the army,

99

when the King gave some of his Amazons as wives to favoured officials, when new laws were passed, old ones repealed.

Although Burton did not see human sacrifice, the beating of the death-drum at night left him in no doubt about what was happening and on his way to take part in the fifth day of the Abomey Customs he witnessed the results. The first change he noticed when he reached the palace square was that one of the victim-sheds was empty. Then he saw a grotesque sight: four corpses, in their red-heart shirts and dunces' caps, were sitting in pairs on wooden stools, kept upright by a double-storeyed scaffold about forty feet high, made of roughly trimmed beams. A short distance away on another double scaffold two victims were hanging, one below the other. Between these was a gallows about thirty feet high from which one corpse was hanging upside down. Farther on, two corpses were tied horizontally along the cross-bar of a gallows. Burton saw no signs of violence on the naked bodies, though they had been mutilated after death 'in respect of the royal wives'.

He went on and found the second victim-hut empty too. On both sides of the entrance lay a dozen heads. 'They were in two batches of six each, disposed in double lines of three. Their faces were downwards, and the cleanly severed necks caught the observer's eye.' Around each heap was a raised rim of white ashes. Within the palace entrance were two more heads, making a total of fourteen. After viewing the corpses Burton and his party took their seats, 'enjoying the fine Harmattanish weather, and were greeted by sundry nobles, who politely thanked us for honouring the day with our uniform'.

This was the day on which the King displayed his wealth. It was a unique exhibition. Forbes, with a meticulousness for detail that for once even outdoes Burton, takes an appendix of thirteen pages to list what he saw. He begins with the procession of women. They numbered nearly two thousand and marched past the King in single file carrying, among a multitude of other things, a carved sheep, a 'horseman clock', glass chandeliers, a silver ostrich with a silver egg under each wing, and one gilt chair. Then came a procession of men who displayed, among other things, a tray containing three human skulls, the King's bath-tub, a live ostrich, a 'large box on four

100

wheels', a landau (English), an umbrella ornamented with eighty human jaw bones, a large wooden horse on wheels, a green chariot, a 'native' sofa and various skulls, jawbones, muskets, banners and umbrellas. After the last lines of men had passed the King it was the turn of the women again and apart from wives, Amazons, etc., who were also part of the King's wealth, Forbes noted 'an English wheeled-chair of the time of Elizabeth', a glass coach, 'Dahomey make', an English family coach, a sarcophagus on wheels, two wooden mounted horsemen on wheels (English made), one head wife, one otto-man of deer skin, six ladies of the chamber, fifty-two chamber utensils 'more useful than ornamental', hundreds of varying-coloured bottles and vases, one washing-pan, dozens of harem-women, one grandmother 'in scarlet and gold' and two women each described as 'another King's widow'—perhaps the skulls of their husbands had preceded them.

Burton spent several hours watching similar processions, but where Forbes had been impressed, he was irritated and wrote that 'almost any pawn-broker's shop could boast a collection more costly'. Yet he found interest enough to make lists nearly as long as Forbes's and among the strangest of the King's possessions listed 'a huge battle-axe perforated like a fish-slicer', two American trotting wagons with leather hoods, a male slave carrying a long blue pole, topped with an imita-tion knife, stained red, and 'a fat sheep with a necklace of cowries and a cloth over its hinder parts', as well as the usual complement of wives, Amazons, soldiers, slaves, skulls, guns, banners and umbrellas.

At the end of the ceremony Burton once more tried to de-liver his message, and once more the King put him off. The bodies were still in place as he made his way back to his house. The heat was already beginning to affect them.

* * *

Burton was allowed a day's rest, then he was plunged into the Customs for the Bush King, *Addo-Kpon*. These were much the same as for the Town King and were held at *Addo-Kpon's* palace about six miles south-west of Abomey. Gelele wanted Burton to fight again for cowries. On the first occasion he had taken the King's invitation seriously and had knocked over the Reverend Bernasko in his eagerness, and it was this diverting spectacle that the King wished to see repeated. Burton refused. However, on the second day Gelele was adamant that the white men do something towards the entertainment and held Burton to his promise of a dancing exhibition. Unabashed, Burton collected his party, tapped out the rhythm he wanted to the Dahomean drummers and performed what he describes as a '*Hindostani pas seul*' which apparently drew tremendous applause. Then the King indicated it was the turn of the Reverend Bernasko to entertain them. It had been agreed that a man of the cloth did not have to dance in a public place so Mr Bernasko devised a different form of entertainment: he conducted a short religious service—a 'God-palaver', as Burton had it. He had a concertina and accompanied himself in hymn-singing for half an hour. One of the hymns, whose irony considering the occasion seems to have been lost on him, was 'All people that on earth do dwell'. A short distance away those in the victim-shed would not be dwelling there very long.

When he had finished the King requested a grand exhibition with Mr Bernasko playing and singing while Mr Cruikshank and Burton danced. 'It was almost too ridiculous,' Burton wrote. 'But we complied for a short time.' He was lucky he only had to dance. John Duncan, an earlier traveller to Dahomey, had to dance before King Gezo and play the Jew's harp at the same time. Burton then danced a second solo which drove the crowd wild with delight and several *caboceers* came to dance around his party. In the midst of all this dust and confusion the Reverend Bernasko, apparently carried away by the moment, was heard to recite:

'O let us be joyful, joyful, joyful,
When we meet to part no more.'

That night was a second *Nox irae*, as Burton called it, when the victims were despatched to the noise of death-drums and musket fire. Again he did not witness any killing. But Skertchly did. He was an enforced guest at the bush King's Customs in

102

1871. This was the infamous *Attoh* Customs which used a platform about 100 feet long by 30 feet wide built outside the palace. Skertchly says that when he attended the Customs there were twenty-six men in the victim-shed bound *à la mode* and sitting on large flat baskets. The ceremony was heralded by a solemn procession of fetish priests and priestesses. 'In the middle was a native of Katu, gagged and bound to one of the baskets in common use by porters, and behind him, lashed to similar baskets, were an alligator, a cat, and a hawk. These were borne on the heads of some of the inferior priests, and a band of horns and drums played a kind of knell in staccato time, something after the fashion of a bell tolling— a few quick notes and then a pause. This sad procession slowly paraded three times round the market . . .

'At the end of the parade they formed before the platform, and cowries, cloth, powder and a gun, were dashed (given) to the victim who, together with the three animals, was then placed upon the heads of some of the Amazons and carried to the platform. A speech was made giving the reason for the forthcoming killing; the man would go to the dead men, the alligator to the fish, the cat to the animals, and the hawk to the birds—to tell of the great things done by Gelele.

'The basket with the unfortunate man upon it was then toppled over the edge of the platform, the poor wretch falling on the hard earth at the foot with a force that, let us hope, stunned him. The basket was then upended, and the executioner for the nonce commenced his horrid work.

'The knife was light, short, and without edge, and after three chops at the neck of the victim without separating the vertebrae, he put the bloody weapon between his teeth and borrowed another heavier knife from a bystander, and with it completed his barbarous work. Sickening as was the spectacle, I was not able to discover the least sign of pity, horror, or disgust on the faces of any of the throng; the monarch alone turning his head away from the fearful sight.' Over the next few days Skertchly was to see this repeated again and again.

Burton did, once more, see the results of the killings for when his party went back to the palace in Abomey the following day the original corpses, which had been badly torn about by buzzards, had been replaced by newly dead bodies. Four were hanging head down, two were lashed in a sitting position and two others in a horizontal state. Burton was assured, as he had been the first time, that these men were criminals and captives. The two corpses lying horizontally had had salt bags forced over their heads as a punishment for stealing the King's salt. In the ground at each side of the palace gate four fresh heads were hidden by little fences of grass.

During the tail-end of the Customs he tried several times to see the King but each time he was put off. 'Time slips easily away at Agbome,' he wrote. 'Rising with the dawn, we set out as soon as the hammockmen can be collected, and walk till nine a.m. Refection follows till eleven, and my lesson in Fon outlasts the noon. If we visit the Komasi Palace the rest of the day will be blank; the brain becomes so weary that work in the evening is impossible. If we avoid it the afternoon is an inverted copy of the forenoon.' It was not until February 20, nearly two months after their arrival, that the King finally saw Burton on his mission. The reason may have been that Dahomey had declared war on Abeokuta and Burton, who had visited the town, was asked to draw its defences; or perhaps it was because he threatened to leave Abomey whether he was 'passed', i.e. given permission to leave, or not.

The meeting was unlike any previous one. Most white people had been in awe of the Dahomean kings; Burton was in awe of no one. They talked for several hours in a room in the palace and although both were polite, neither minced words and each went through a phase of anger, a 'stirring of the mind', in the Fon phrase. Burton began by complaining that he had been kept waiting for two months; the King replied that he had been busy with his Customs. Burton complained that he had not been allowed to move freely about Dahomey or journey to the Makhi mountains for sport and recreation. The King asked whether roaming around Dahomey and enjoying sport and recreation in the mountains were contained in his orders from the Foreign Office. When Burton admitted that they were not, the King assured him that if he had been ordered to move about freely he would have been allowed to do so. Burton must have experienced a 'stirring of the mind' just then for he says that Gelele waited until his brow cleared before asking him to read the message. This was largely the same as all the others sent over the years by the British Government: Would the King please stop slavery and end the ritual killings. And the King's reply was equally old: he said that the slave trade was an ancestral custom established by white men to whom he would sell all they wanted. In any case the traditions of his kingdom compelled him to make war; and unless he sold off the prisoners he must kill them: would the British Government like that any better? Of the sacrifices he said that he only killed criminals or war captives who, if they could, would do the same to him. He asked for Burton's comments on these matters and was told that nude and mutilated corpses were a disgusting sight and that Burton would advise all Englishmen who wished to avoid 'tickling of the liver' (nausea) to keep away from Dahomey. This apparently stirred the King's mind and he complained bitterly about the Royal Navy interfering with his shipping. They had reached an impasse and one imagines them glowering at each other in silence with the Reverend Bernasko, who had accompanied him, caught in the middle and fearful for his life.

Abruptly, the King said the meeting was over. Burton wrote: 'He told me that if my mind was no longer stirred we might drink together. I again denied personal bad feeling towards him . . . (we) drank gin and liqueur. The King then arose to conduct us outside the palace. The inner doorway being too narrow for two abreast, I fell back a little, and he asked the reason, through the interpreter. My answer was, with us crowned heads always walk first; whereupon he shook hands cordially, told me that I was a "good man, but", rolling his head, "too angry". At the distance of 200 yards he stood, shook hands, snapped fingers, and bade us adieu, exhorting a speedy return.

But Burton never did return. The following day he left for the coast where a cruiser was waiting to pick him up.

8

ON THE day Burton left Abomey, the Dahomean army, led by Gelele, marched on Abeokuta. It took them twenty-two days—on twelve of which they marched from 6 a.m. to 2 p.m., on ten of which they rested—to cover the 120 miles between the two capitals. They marched in four battalions, the total force being estimated at between ten and twelve thousand, and were almost starving by the time they reached the Ogun River. On March 15, 1864, they crossed the river near Abeokuta, floating three old cannons—one bore the legend, 'Mexico, 1815'— with them. Though it was early in the morning and foggy, they were soon spotted by the Egbas and a warning cannon was fired to wake the town. When the Dahomeans came in sight of the walls they found them lined with muskets and the Egbas awaiting the attack unafraid. The Dahomeans came on, making for the gate at which King Gezo had been beaten back in an earlier war but the Egbas had dug a series of tunnel defences and now four hundred young warriors poured out through these passages on to the plain and barred the Dahomeans' path. The Dahomeans altered course and reached a point about two hundred yards from the walls of the town when the battle began. The Dahomeans charged the walls but were stopped by musket-fire from above, and many took cover in the dry moat. Amid the smoke and flying ball the Amazons stormed the walls in a furious charge, only to be dragged over the top by the defenders and cut to pieces. Some crept through the tunnels but were decapitated by the waiting Egbas. It is said that one Amazon, who had lost an arm in the escalade, shot an Egba with the other before being speared to death. Three other Amazons were cut down and their heads and hands exhibited on poles.

The battle lasted for about an hour and a half when the Dahomeans withdrew. They had lost between eighty and a hundred soldiers on the walls, the Egbas fifteen. The long march, the lack of food and the powerful Egba defences combined to demoralize the Dahomean army and they began to retreat on the Ogun River valley. The Egbas came after them and soon the retreat became a rout. All cohesion was lost. Order was replaced by chaos. Officers could no longer control their men or women. Battalions split up into small groups which were hunted down mercilessly by the Egbas. What made everything worse was that it was the end of the dry weather and none of the small streams contained water. The Dahomeans fled through the bush, many dropping from hunger and thirst. Between four and five hundred Dahomean prisoners were butchered by the Egbas on the spot because they were too weak and exhausted to travel back to Abeokuta. Many had walked and run more than thirty-five miles by nightfall. The Dahomean loss was fearful. One estimate put the total number of dead at more than six thousand, which was half the Dahomean army. The Egbas cut all the bodies to bits. It is said that every Egba, man and woman, who passed a Dahomean corpse, slashed or stoned it. Commenting on the defeat, Burton wrote: 'According to the latest accounts, the incorrigible king at once bought a number of slaves and returned to his capital a conqueror.'

* * *

The Reverend Bernasko reported that Gelele once said that 'his father was a king of blacks and a friend of whites; but himself is a king of both'. Burton would never have agreed. He despised Gelele as he did all blacks and often disparaged his actions, especially his defeat at Abeokuta which he compared unfavourably with the much braver stand—though it also ended in defeat—by his father Gezo in 1851. And it is true that Abeokuta was Gelele's Moscow. He tried another attack in 1871 and took another beating. But Abeokuta was the exception; apart from that he was a most successful warlord and one scholar has estimated that of thirteen expeditions against a total of fifty-three towns and villages he captured 5,800 prisoners and 2,300 heads. In the pantheon of Dahomean kings he is one of the best-remembered, both for his success in war and for his skill in allegory and metaphor, and as late as 1911 his sayings were still employed by the Fon people as the best means of illustrating their history.

It was Gelele's misfortune that his reign coincided with an awakening world conscience and also, of course, with the scramble for Africa. By 1863 the French had obtained protectorate rights on Porto Novo. In 1868 they signed a treaty with Gelele's viceroy in Whydah which ceded them the beach at Cotonu. There was pressure from the Portuguese to get a toehold on the coast. Everyone wanted a share of the palm oil trade. It is hardly surprising that there were conflicts of interest between whites and between whites and blacks. In 1876 the first dispute arose with the Europeans. A group of chiefs arrested the Whydah agent of the English firm of Swansea and Company after a quarrel over certain goods. Although he was soon released he informed the Royal Navy, which took an extreme imperialistic view of the case and demanded from Gelele heavy compensation in palm oil for insulting an English subject. The King refused. The Navy blockaded the coast and trade suffered. Gelele, brooding in Abomey, said that he had no need of European goods anyway and threatened to block the roads to Whydah, thus wrecking trade entirely. The white traders on the coast became fearful of being ruined financially and after seven months of blockade they themselves paid the compensation and the blockade was lifted. But the lesson was clear. Big commercial concerns had invested too much in Dahomey for their governments to take this sort of thing casually. Portugal abandoned any claim on Dahomey. The French signed more treaties with the viceroy. The country began to split in two: the chiefs on the coast dealt on the spot with white commercial interests, signing away land and rights; the King in Abomey, not comprehending the nature of the treaties, was unwilling to allow their implementation. It is basically the same story as occurred elsewhere in Africa. The whites, because of their philosophy on property and ownership, failed to comprehend that the land was not divisible, could not be shared out or sold or lent; it belonged to the people in the symbol of the King. So when the French prepared to assert what they thought were their rights at Cotonu and suggested that Gelele give up certain dues and accept a pension, he told the French representative that he would never give up his rights at Cotonu, that the *yegovan* (viceroy) and the *caboceers* who had signed the treaties had had their heads removed and that he recognized no treaties he had not signed himself.

The French decided to send a mission to Abomey to treat with the King. When it arrived Gelele was ill and he died on December 31, 1889—with nothing agreed. With him, for all intents and purposes, died the Dahomean monarchy. He was succeeded by Behanzin, who also refused to surrender what he regarded as his inalienable rights over Cotonu. There were skirmishes between Dahomeans and French. Then Behanzin, in keeping with Dahomean war tradition, attacked a group of tribes which the French considered were in their sphere of influence. They told Behanzin to keep off. The King described their letter as an insult. Dahomean soldiers next fired on a French river steamer without orders from the King. The French mustered an expeditionary force. Behanzin tried to parley, but his letters were ignored. On August 10, 1892, the French bombarded Whydah and several other towns and advanced on Abomey. The Amazons fought tigerishly but the French were too well armed. However, the female battalions managed to delay the advance long enough for Behanzin to burn down Abomey and his palace with it so that it would not fall into French hands.

The expeditionary force camped near the ruins of the town while negotiations proceeded with Behanzin. At last, on January 25, 1894, the King gave himself up after the French had accepted a puppet king called Ago-li-agbo, who was to rule under their authority. Dahomey thus became part of the French colonial empire until it was granted independence in 1960. It is an independent republic, which would have depressed Burton were he alive now. For he was intransigent to the last. Writing about the defeat of Gelele at Abeokuta, his book ends:

'Many years must lapse before Dahome [sic] can recover from the blow, and before that time I hope to see her level with the ground.' If losing her freedom to French colonial interests meant being 'level with the ground', he must have been well satisfied. But it is odd to reflect that had Burton been black, he would probably have ruled Dahomey precisely as Gelele had done, if not more ferociously. Indeed, it would have been impossible to do otherwise: the mould had been formed hundreds of years before when the whites put pressure on Africa, the black mother, for her children.

PART THREE

'The Lice in the Queen's Blanket'

'Whoever feels for the native and cares for his future must wish a fair chance for the experiment now being tried in Basutoland, of letting him develop in his own way, shielded from the rude pressure of the whites.'
—James Bryce. *Impressions of South Africa.* 1898.

Basuto warrior dressed for battle

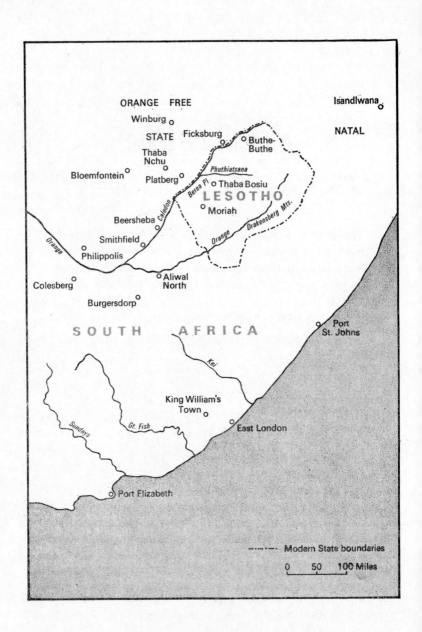

ORANGE FREE

Winburg

STATE   Ficksburg

Buthe-
Buthe

Thaba
Nchu

Phuthiatsana

Bloemfontein   Platberg

Thaba Bosiu

Berea Pl   LESOTHO

Moriah

Caledon

Beersheba

Drakensberg Mts.

Smithfield

Orange

Orange

Philippolis

Colesberg   Aliwal
North

Burgersdorp

SOUTH   AFRICA

Port
St. Johns

Kei

King William's
Town

East London

Sundays   Gt. Fish

Port Elizabeth

Isandlwana

NATAL

Modern State boundaries

0   50   100 Miles

1

I<small>N</small> T<small>HE</small> early 1820s a catastrophe fell upon a large part of southern Africa. From the east coast of what is now Natal across the high central plateau of the country to the edge of the Kalahari Desert, inter-tribal warfare broke out on a scale never experienced before; twenty-eight tribes were wiped out, others were fractured into family units and absorbed by other tribes. Villages were burnt and crops and cattle looted to feed rampaging armies. In a few years the countryside became a tawny wasteland over which moved a host of broken men in search of food. Cannibalism, almost unknown in these regions, became rife: husbands ate their wives, mothers their children.

This was a purely black phenomenon and the few whites who had penetrated thus far into the interior by that time, missionaries and traders, a few hunters, were the only foreign witnesses. No one knows how many people died during the years that followed, but one historian puts the figure at two million. The shock of the period on those involved was so great that it caused the very roots of black society to wither. Yet, out of this chaos only a few years later was to emerge a unique black kingdom which still exists. Extraordinary as these two factors are in themselves, what is almost beyond credibility is that Lesotho, or Basutoland as it was called in the colonial period, should exist how and where it does: an independent black state lying in the middle of South Africa.

It owes its existence in the main to one black man, one white man and a not-very-impressive hill. The black man, the father of the Basuto nation, was called Moshesh,[1] the white man was a French missionary, Eugene Casalis, and the

---

[1] The spelling of Bantu names has undergone changes in recent years. Moshesh is now spelt in a variety of ways, Mosheshwe or Moshoeshoe being the most common. The name means 'the shaver', i.e. the man who shaves his neighbours clean—of cattle. I have kept to the simple spelling forms wherever possible. Lesotho is the name of the country, Basuto the people, Mosuto a single person and Sesuto the language they speak.

hill was—and still is—called Thaba Bosiu, the Mountain of Night.

Lesotho is a long way, both physically and emotionally, from the banana trees and hot savannahs of Dahomey, and the fever valleys of the Old Kingdom. Here are no coloured 'kidey-solls', no courtly pageantry, no Annual Customs, no slavery, no furs and tippets from Portugal, no black dukes or bixcomdes. They are two different worlds. Though Lesotho lies to the south of both, it is in a sense a more 'northern' country than either.

It is a land of snow-capped mountains, of bleak, treeless uplands, of savage winters and unpredictable summers where snow has been known to fall on Christmas Day. It is about the size of Belgium but the country it has most often been compared to is Switzerland. There is a similarity, but with a Switzerland of the past: of lost and isolated valleys and of endless mountains—the highest in southern Africa—rising and falling in waves of brown winter grass. Its people dressed themselves in animal skins and furs and lived in small villages of mud and thatch. They spent much of their time in summer attempting to steal their neighbours' cattle, and much of the winter crouched over eye-watering fires of dried dung.

As the Bushmen had found years before when they were hunted from their lairs near the Cape of Good Hope, it was a good country for hiding in. Even today many of its valleys are almost inaccessible, its mountains are often natural fortresses with flat tops guarded by steep cliffs; there are caves everywhere. In a sense Lesotho is itself a fastness, a fortress, a land–island towering out of the plains of South Africa. It was towards this fastness that thousands of homeless refugees made their way in the late 1820s. Until that time it had been almost uninhabited, there was no Basuto nation.

Moshesh was in his late thirties by the time the tribal wars —the *difaqane* or 'forced migrations', as the period is known— began. He came out of nowhere. His father, Mokachane, was a simple village headman. In his youth and early manhood Moshesh gave little evidence of the man to come. He was a cattle reiver in the tradition of his people, but slightly more daring than his contemporaries. Because of this he attracted a small following. At this time the Caledon River Valley,

114

where he had been born, was comparatively thickly populated by small clans of Basuto, each governed by a chief who was constantly contracting alliances with or fighting against one or other of the neighbouring clans. There was no overall power and a 'war' between two clans was little more than a raid which, though it might result in the loss of large numbers of cattle, did not cause much loss of life.

Moshesh was pursuing this mode of life with a future no more or less bright than any other petty headman's son, when he underwent a seminal experience: he met a chief called Mohlomi, who had garnered a wide reputation as a philosopher, wandering prophet, rainmaker and benign wizard. He was also what one historian has called a 'practical polygamist', who married into ruling families wherever he went, settled cattle on his bride and went on his way. Mohlomi was uncharacteristic of his place and time, for he practised as well as preached a wide tolerance, showed goodwill to all, detested war and constantly inveighed against it. Some time before his death he completely converted Moshesh, a considerable feat, for the size of a chief's following depended upon the amount of food he could provide, which in turn meant his success as a raider. It is a measure of Moshesh's genius for compromise that he was able to graft Mohlomi's new concepts on to the traditional Basuto way of life, yet still win an increasing number of followers. By the year 1822 when the *difaqane* began, he was a minor chief ruling a small clan in a part of the world few, if any, white men had penetrated.

Less than two hundred miles to the north-east another minor chief had gathered a following and was committed to expanding his vassalage and his territory. This was the Zulu king, Shaka, an almost exact contemporary of Moshesh's. The date for Shaka's birth is given as 1787 and that for Moshesh as about 1786. The effect of Shaka's rise to power on Moshesh was to be enormous.

Shaka had become the Zulu king in 1817 by means of treachery and murder, and immediately began to reorganize this small and insignificant east-Nguni tribe. By the time he had finished it had become the most famous fighting machine in the black world. Shaka dispensed with the long throwing spear that was most commonly used in battle and introduced the short stabbing spear. This meant a fundamental change in battle tactics. Instead of facing an enemy on a long front and throwing missiles at him, the Zulu army now attacked at close quarters, using a pincer movement that was likened to the head and horns of a bull, the head containing the shock troops who bore the brunt of a frontal attack, the horns closing around the flanks of the enemy and preventing his escape. With these tactics Shaka's *impis* proved unstoppable. What happened when the Zulus exploded from their small tribal area in search of *Lebensraum*, cattle and new citizens had the most profound effect on millions of blacks who had never even heard his name. It was like dropping a stone into the centre of a pond; but here the outward-flowing ripples overtook each other. Tribe after tribe fled from the Zulus, each in turn falling on a neighbouring tribe, that tribe on the next, the next upon the next, and so on across South Africa: the 'forced migrations' had begun.

One of the most infamous hordes produced by these swelling circles of destruction was the Mantatees.[1] They comprised portions of several clans but mainly those of the Batlokwa (the People of the Wild Cat) who had fled westward over the Drakensberg Mountains. This horde, swollen to about fifty thousand, rolled across the country, killing and looting until they reached the fringe of the Kalahari Desert near the Batlapin town of Litakun. Here they were faced by a small force of one hundred well-armed and well-mounted Griquas, and five hundred Batlapin warriors.

The Reverend Robert Moffat, a missionary at Kuruman, has left an account of this meeting. He was riding with a reconnaissance party of ten Griquas under their chief Waterboer when they came in sight of part of the huge horde—about fifteen thousand—in a ravine near Litakun. The remainder, about thirty-five thousand, had occupied the town itself. Not all of these, of course, were fighting men, for the Mantatees marched much as the Persians had marched under Darius and Xerxes, with their women—and in this case children as well.

[1] They took their name from their formidable leader, a woman called MaNantatisi who was said to have only one eye in the middle of her forehead and whose warriors were said to suckle at her huge, pendulous breasts.

116

When the battle was joined the Griquas employed tactics that the Voortrekkers were to use successfully a few years later against attacks by Bantu armies: with the advantage of being mounted they were able to advance to fire, and retire to reload, and yet remain all the while outside the range of the spears. For several hours this one-sided warfare continued. The Griquas were using heavy muskets and each ball fired into the densely packed throng would have injured more than one person. The Mantatees, unable to get to grips with the elusive Griquas, set fire to Litakun and began to move out of the town. It must have been a wild sight: the flames leaping up from the burning thatch of the huts, the black smoke rising in pillars, the great clouds of dust set up by thousands of bare feet, and the Griqua horsemen riding the perimeter, firing at will. The two sections of Mantatees now joined together forming a host five hundred yards long and one hundred yards wide. As they retreated, the Batlapins, who had taken little part in the battle, swooped down from the neighbouring heights and fell like wolves on the wounded, the women and the children, hacking some to pieces with their war axes to get at bangles and ornaments.

Moffat wrote: 'The wounded and dying did not manifest those signs of sensibility which the situation was calculated to draw forth. The cries of infants who had fallen from the arms of their flying or slaughtered mothers, were distinctly heard; but the others seemed but little affected by their woeful situation. A ferocious thirst for vengeance seemed to reign paramount in the breasts of the dying warriors. Several times I narrowly escaped the spears and battle axes of the wounded, while engaged in rescuing the women and children. Men, struggling with death, would raise themselves from the ground, and throw their weapons with the utmost fury at any one of us who approached them. Their vengeful spirit seemed to be subdued only when life was extinct. Instead of laying down their arms, and suing for quarter, some actually fought on their knees, their legs being broken!

'Many of the Mantatees, especially the women and the infirm, appeared to be suffering dreadfully from famine. Most of the prisoners were much exhausted, and exceedingly ravenous for food; and the dead warriors looked lean and gaunt, though in battle they had displayed amazing agility and swiftness. About five hundred bodies of the enemy lay scattered over the field of battle—so destructive had been the Griqua muskets; while on our side not one man was killed and only one slightly wounded. One Bechuana (Batlapin) lost his life, being slain (a fate richly merited) by one of the wounded whom he was plundering.'

The Mantatees journeyed back across the High Veld the way they had come, resumed their old name of Batlokwa and settled near Moshesh. At that time his stronghold was a steep-sided hill near Buthe-Buthe in the Caledon Valley. MaNantatisi settled her people just north of the river near the present town of Ficksburg. Her policy was to gather as many people under her leadership as she could and extend her territory as far as possible. But that was also Moshesh's policy and he was in her way. Her army, under the leadership of her son, a young but brutal warrior called Sikonyela, began to harass Moshesh, whose store of food in his hill fort dwindled to a dangerously low level. In desperation he sent out runners to find a stronghold farther away from the Batlokwa. When they returned they described a hill about sixty miles to the south-west which stood in an isolated valley and which, though it was not very high, appeared to be strong enough to withstand an attack. Moshesh moved his whole tribe, now about two thousand strong, with their cattle, by a circuitous route through remote valleys eluding the Batlokwa outposts. But the mountains were infested with cannibals and several of the tribe who could not keep up were attacked and eaten, including Moshesh's own grandfather, Peete. Moshesh finally reached his destination late one afternoon and by nightfall the entire tribe with its cattle were on the hilltop. This has been advanced as the reason the hill was called Thaba Bosiu—the Mountain of Night.

There can be few mountains which have played so vital a role in the history of a people as Thaba Bosiu—one thinks of Masada on the Dead Sea or Magdala in Ethiopia. Had Moshesh had the choice of any hill in southern Africa he could not have done better. It is insignificant when one first sees it. It lies on the Phuthiatsana River and is only about 350 feet at its highest point. The top, which is almost completely flat, is some 150 acres in extent and has an abundant spring of water. The whole flat area—good enough grazing for short periods of siege—is guarded by cliffs which drop away just below the summit and completely surround it. There are six fissures which give access to the top but of these only three might be considered possible by an attacking army. They are called the Khubelu, the Mokachane and the Raebe passes. Moshesh built his own huts above the first and placed those of his father, Mokachane, above the second. The Raebe Pass was suitable for launching rocks, so great piles were gathered near the top, some of which still remain. The hill was a natural fortress, better than a Crusader castle; it could withstand a siege in conditions far less insanitary and therefore less liable to disease. Today Thaba Bosiu is deserted. It is the burial mound of the Basuto kings and as such it is a sacred place.

By the beginning of 1827, three years after the move to the new fortress, Moshesh's tribe had expanded to about three thousand, part living on the top of the hill and part around the base. Like Shaka, MaNantatisi and several other chiefs, Moshesh had given succour to many refugees. He was prospering. He was far enough away from the Batlokwa to feel reasonably safe. His most dangerous enemy, Shaka, died about this time, murdered by his half-brother, Dingane, to whom Moshesh paid a tribute of young maidens, skins and feathers in exchange for peace. For a while the peace endured, but no one expected it to last for ever.

The first of many attacks on Thaba Bosiu came not from either the Zulus or the Batlokwas but from a tribe of Zulu origin called the Amangwane who had landed up on the Caledon River as a result of the *difaqane*. Moshesh was already paying tribute to their chief, Matiwane, but it is said that Matiwane objected to the Basutos paying tribute to the Zulus as well. This may have only been an excuse, for Moshesh's cattle had been increasing even faster than his tribe, and cattle were wealth. Whatever the reason, Matiwane decided to attack Thaba Bosiu in July, 1827. The Amangwane approached the fortress from a high plateau called the Berea from which one can actually look down on Thaba Bosiu. Then they had to descend the plateau and cross the Phuthiatsana

River before reaching the base of the hill. The Amangwanes, fielding six divisions and greatly outnumbering the Basutos, attacked in almost complete surprise. But two of the Basuto 'war doctors' were just in time to confine them to a comparatively narrow front by bewitching several of the river crossings which the superstitious Amangwane then refused to use. Moshesh at first attacked the enemy below Thaba Bosiu, causing severe damage. When other elements of the Amangwane tried to storm the heights they were destroyed by a shower of rock avalanches. In the midst of this Moshesh ordered a counter-attack. It was too much for Matiwane's forces, who began streaming back up the Berea plateau, passing caches of beer which they had brought to celebrate their anticipated victory.

Four years later, Moshesh faced another critical challenge: he was attacked by Moselekatze and his highly trained Matabele *impis*. Moselekatze, a Zulu clan chief, had broken with Shaka and fled from Zululand nearly ten years before. During that time he had outdone his former master in acts of cruelty. He had crossed the Drakensberg westward and cut a bloody swathe through what is now the Transvaal. When Shaka pursued him he began a scorched earth policy that laid waste hundreds of square miles and aggravated the existing famine. After a while he swung south and on a day in March, 1831, Moshesh, standing on Thaba Bosiu, saw the approaching regiments. He knew that these Matabele warriors were veterans, battle-trained and battle-hard, and wisely decided to fight them from a defensive position and not take his army down on to the plains. The Matabeles topped to rest on the banks of the Phuthiatsana River, sharpening their spears and seeing to their feathered head-dresses. Moshesh used this time to build up huge mounds of rocks at the top of his hill passes.

The Matabele attacked twice up the steep fissures and each time were driven from the slope by plunging boulders. It was a form of warfare they had not encountered before and for which they had no answer. After bitter recriminations and allegations of cowardice they began to drift away to the north. Now Moshesh showed the qualities that were to distinguish him throughout his life, qualities that any international statesman might have envied. He sent a herd of cattle down to Moselekatze with the message that these were for his men so that they would not be hungry on their long march back to the Transvaal. Moshesh was never again attacked by the Matabele, but that did not mean his Basuto were to be left in peace.

From 1830 they had to contend with a different kind of enemy, the Koranas, a tribe of Hottentot blood who, though professing Christianity, lived by the booty they could collect plundering weaker tribes. Like their cousins the Griquas who had fought so well against the Mantatees, the Koranas, though few in number, were well armed and well mounted. Most were first-class shots. Acting in small bodies they would leave their huts, cover forty or fifty miles in a night, dismount at dawn outside one of the Basuto villages that were now being built farther and farther from Thaba Bosiu as the population increased, shoot down the warriors, who could not reach them with their assegais, kill the women, drive off the stock, and leave. Their weakness was liquor: they drank it wherever they found it and they often found it in these villages. It was usually a heavy beer made from local millet and it was because of the Koranas' predilection for this beverage that the Basutos had their first successes against them. They would wait until the Koranas were stupefied by drink, kill them and then watch their horses for hours until they were sure that the explosion of the muskets had not come from these strange beasts, which they have never seen before.

The Koranas were no real threat to Moshesh but their tactics set him thinking. He had seen how impotent his warriors were against the musket and the horse and decided never to be at such a disadvantage again if it could be avoided. It would be difficult to overemphasize the importance of this decision. It made the Basuto, certainly as far as horses were concerned, unique among Bantu tribes so that when they were later to meet the armies of white nations they could do so on some level of equality. This could not even be said of the Zulus—in spite of their victory at Isandlwana—for they kept to the old weapons and old ways which had stood them in good stead against their black neighbours but which had little relevance to the increasingly sophisticated weapons of the whites. Until the Basuto captured horses from the Koranas, their warriors had gone to war on foot dressed in a leather kilt, a brass gorget round the neck and a ball of feathers on the head. For arms they used shields of hardened leather, spears and light throwing axes. It took several years before they had a nucleus of horses to breed from. When they did a new type of horse, the famous Basuto pony, emerged. It was small but it was able to endure hardship and in the mountains it was as sure-footed as a goat.

But this was in the future and for the moment Moshesh and his tribe had to endure on their hilltop surrounded by thousands of starving people, many of whom had turned cannibal.

Moshesh was as much to blame for this state of affairs as anyone, and he knew it. In 1843, in the presence of a group of cannibals led by a bushy-browed giant called Rakotsoane— the very group that had eaten Moshesh's grandfather, Peete— he said, 'We, the masters of the country, did drive you to live on human flesh for men cannot eat stones. You ate my father but before that I had eaten yours.' (Meaning all their means of subsistence.)

Cannibalism, according to a French missionary, the Reverend D. G. Ellenberger, spread from the Orange River to the Vaal, depopulating the land and stopping all friendly intercourse between tribes and villages. Murder and robbery were rife, people only dared to move in large armed parties. How easy it was to change the nature of people to whom cannibalism was quite foreign was shown by what happened to a tribe called the Bafokeng. Once a powerful people, the forced migrations had left them frail and frightened. Moshesh in a moment of weakness gave in to pressure from his brother Mohale and allowed him to raid the Bafokeng for whatever cattle they had left. Mohale took everything and the Bafokeng were left utterly destitute. They adopted cannibalism as the only means of saving themselves, killing and eating any travellers they could ambush. In each case, they flayed the victim and dressed the skin as they might have done an animal hide, then made clothing for the women and breech-cloths for the men.

Moshesh's people were one of only three Basuto clans who

did not become cannibals and the other two saved themselves either by moving into the Cape Colony or being lucky enough to live in an area so remote as to be inaccessible.

Mr Ellenberger, who made a special study of cannibalism in Lesotho, wrote: 'It must be remembered that in the early days the staple food of a pastoral people was milk supplemented by grain. Therefore when the invasions came, and the cattle were captured by the enemy, people had to fly from their homes and fields, cultivation ceased, and they were in grievous case. Even the game, which had been abundant, disappeared before the invading hordes, but the beasts of prey remained, and throve exceedingly on the liberal diet so lavishly provided for them. Women with babies on their backs, dragging little children along with them when flying before the enemy, have testified how they had to abandon their offspring to wild beasts, or wilder men, when they were unable to follow any longer; and how they themselves escaped at the cost of cruel sufferings, subsisting for weeks on water and roots, if on nothing worse. One wretched woman, when converted, sobbed, "I am indeed a murderess, for I have eaten the fruit of my own womb."

'Cannibalism as practised by the Basuto was indeed a madness. All human instinct, all reason, fellowship, intellect, everything in fact which raises the human being over the brute beast, became extinct or obliterated. They practised cruelty for its own sake and the pleasure it gave them, torturing their victims in a fiendish manner before despatching them. Children were butchered or roasted alive under the eyes of their parents, or vice versa; women in the presence of their husbands. They would bind the hands of captured people, and drive them before them as they would cattle. If any one resisted, he was killed and eaten at once, to save the trouble of driving him. The women of the cannibals were just as blood-thirsty. They would frequently accompany their husbands on the man-hunt, so as to miss no part of the feast.

'When, as it sometimes happened, many victims were captured at one time, the fattest was eaten first, and the lean ones were forced to eat the flesh in order to fatten them. Sometimes a young woman would be spared for sexual purposes. One such, a tall, thin woman, lived to relate her

123

experiences. She was captured with some others near Teyateya-neng, and driven to a cave near Cana, where all who were in good condition were devoured that evening. She, however, was spared for the purpose stated, and later on escaped. If no victims were forthcoming, wives and children were eaten, but, owing to superstition, not as a rule by their own husbands or fathers. It was thought better to exchange them for others. But this was not always possible; and, if he were hungry, the scruples of the cannibal would speedily be overcome, whether the victim was wife, child, or comrade.'

During the 1830s a French missionary estimated the number of practising cannibals between the Orange River, the Drakensberg and the Vaal at between seven and eight thousand. Ellenberger put the figure low at four thousand and estimated that if each one ate one person a month it would make a total of forty-eight thousand eaten during one year. During the six worst years from 1822 to 1828 this would mean that more than a quarter of a million were eaten.

Cannibalism not only devastated the land but also produced difficulties of a more domestic nature. For instance, when Moshesh's eldest son reached the age of seventeen, it was high time that he was circumcised but it was not possible for him to undergo the rite while his grandfather's grave (he had been eaten) remained in a state of defilement. Moshesh put his agile mind to work and came up with a solution. He summoned Rakotsoane and his cannibals and caused all of them to be rubbed with a special mixture which would purify them. In other words, he was treating them all, for the purposes of the purification ceremony, as the tomb of the departed. At the time several of his chiefs urged him to kill Rakotsoane and his cannibals. Moshesh refused, replying, 'I must consider well before I disturb the sepulchre of my ancestor.'

This, then, was the state of affairs in a country which as yet had no name and no geographical boundaries—the defining and keeping of which was to cause almost all the future trouble—when a man arrived with two companions to preach the gospel to the Basuto. His name was Eugene Casalis and he had been sent out to South Africa by the Evangelical Missionary Society in Paris. It is doubtful whether any nation has been as lucky with its missionaries as the Basuto were with these Frenchmen who followed each other from Paris over the next fifty years. Unlike the perfervid monks and friars who arrived in the Old Kingdom to proselytize with one hand and slave with the other, whose legacy was the horrible irony of a black puppet king executing a black woman and child for committing a heresy against a white religion; unlike Burton, whose contempt for King Gelele and all things negroid was to entrench the very customs he had been asked to try to change—and unlike so many priests, missionaries, immigrants, hunters, farmers and prospectors who tried to shape the country to their own needs—the members of the Paris Evangelical Mission came to Africa wanting nothing from her in exchange for what they hoped to give. The fact that they were Protestant missionaries, themselves a persecuted race in Roman Catholic France, almost certainly gave them a quality in dealing with blacks in Africa that no other missionaries possessed. In his book, *The Rise of the Basuto*, G. Tylden flatly states: 'It is hardly possible to overestimate the value of the work of the mission in Basutoland ... the Basuto owe to it in no small measure their place in the world, their language, their literature, the preservation of their tradition and history, their share in the education they so much desire, and an example of everything that should make up the life of the tribe.'

It was, perhaps, the very best time for missionaries. The anti-slavery movement was in full flood; men's consciences had been stirred. While missionaries were often unpopular in the countries to which they were called they retained a firm grip on the liberal mind in Europe. No one, least of all politicians, could afford to offend the all-powerful Aborigines Protection Society which actively supported the Protestant missions. Neither governments nor their army commanders could any longer ignore missionary opinion. Moshesh was soon to have access to this powerful group in Europe through the French missionaries in his country, and especially through Casalis, who has often been called his 'foreign minister'.

2

EUGENE CASALIS wrote two books about his years
in Lesotho; both are classics of their kind *The Basuto*,
is the most important early work on the people and
country. The other, *My Life In Basuto-land*, is a personal
portrait of a young man transparently idealistic, deeply
religious, easily touched, very emotional, with a great need
to love and be loved—and yet possessed of a streak of French
bourgeois toughness without which he could never have
survived in Africa.

He was born in the town of Orthez in the Basses Pyrénées
in south-western France in November, 1812, of a comfortably-
off Protestant family whose ancestors had lived through the
dangerous times following the Revocation of the Edict of
Nantes. His grandfather, a man of deep convictions, had used
his house as a refuge for the 'pastors of the Desert', the
Protestant ministers who in the time of Huguenot persecution
travelled secretly around France holding illegal services. His
grandmother had been taken from her parents when she was
seven by a *lettre de cachet* and shut up in an Ursuline convent
at Pau until she was eighteen. She reverted to Protestantism
and also took up the dangerous business of helping to keep the
faith alive.

It is not surprising in view of this romantic background
and of the extreme piety in which Casalis was reared that he
should have been drawn to the Church, although he quite
candidly stated that his very first leaning towards religion,
when he was seven, was because he dreaded death and hell.

He was not much older when he realized there were people
in the world with black skins. He wrote, 'Already there began
to show itself in me that love for the coloured races that seemed
almost innate. When I saw a negro or mulatto, which, indeed,
rarely happened, I felt towards him a lively sympathy. I
wanted to stop him, to get him to seat himself by me and
tell me his history. This taste seemed the more remarkable as
these people, at that time so little known in our small provincial towns, were the objects there of a special repugnance.

I attributed my feelings towards them to the emotion which had been awakened in me by reading a history of the conquest of Mexico. A missionary's romance, entitled *Gamul and Leria*, had also made me shed tears over its description of the sufferings of two little Africans, and over the picture it gave of their happiness after they had become converted.'

He studied classics and theology with a tutor in Bayonne and then joined the Evangelical Missionary Society in Paris when he was eighteen. So far he had led a somewhat sheltered life. This changed in Paris. Cholera, which had been creeping across Europe from Asia, finally reached the city in spite of a *cordon sanitaire*. One Saturday evening rumour spread through the streets that a cook had died of the disease. The following day Casalis, an apprentice, was preaching a sermon when a member of the congregation collapsed. 'I descended precipitately from the pulpit', wrote Casalis, 'and held him in my arms. His vomitings covered my clothes. We carried him away. A doctor was sent for. Two hours later poor Postry (his name has always remained with me) was no more; and the next day when I conducted his funeral, his coffin was laid in the midst of twenty others.

'In the course of some weeks we saw thousands fall at our right hand and our left; but at the Mission House not one was touched. Every evening as we went to bed in the dormitory, we embraced each other as though for the last time.' When the epidemic diminished, Casalis and a co-missionary, Arbousset, with whom he was to go to Africa, slogged over the country roads of France carrying the Protestant message to remote villages and cut-off communities. It was hard work struggling through mud and often snow but it was to stand him in good stead for the trials to come.

In 1830 France had conquered Algiers and Casalis and Arbousset were set to work to learn Arabic. Then suddenly the Cape of Good Hope began to be discussed. Casalis was not pleased. 'We had very comfortably settled down to the idea of a field of labour whose distance from home was an affair only of hours,' he wrote. They started to learn Dutch. Soon Casalis went to Orthez to spend two months with his family before setting off. His father had what they thought was chronic gastritis—he was, in fact, dying of stomach cancer—and the eight weeks were fraught with the unspoken spectre of parents and child never seeing each other again. Casalis vividly described the final leave-taking.

'A moment after we were in the saddle, and had gone some steps, I heard my father calling me back.

'"Descend," said he; "I must embrace you once more."

'"No, I beseech you. We shall lose what little strength we still have left."

'"I command you!"'

'I threw myself again into his arms, and he clasped me to his breast in a convulsive embrace, gasping in a broken voice, which went to my heart, 'I shall never see you again here below!"' It was two hours before Casalis could stop sobbing.

He and Arbousset were ordained in 1832 and immediately set off for London where they were joined by M. Gossellin, a stone-mason from Amiens who was to accompany them as an 'artisan missionary'. They sailed from Gravesend in November. Casalis was nineteen years old.

* * *

In 1832 the Cape Colony was on the threshold of huge physical and emotional changes. It had been in British hands since 1806 and during that time the white population had greatly expanded. The interior of the country was little known by the outside world. A few farmers had settled just north of the Orange River, hunters and missionaries somewhat farther. On the eastern side of the country farmers of Boer and British stock confronted the southward-moving Xhosa pastoralists, both sides laying claim to areas of good grazing land. Already there had been wars between black and white, and there would be more to come.

The event which was to change everything was still two years off: the emancipation of all slaves in the British Empire was scheduled for 1834 but was casting a long shadow. Farmers in the Cape were worried about labour shortages and were incensed that the British Government had agreed to pay compensation to slave owners only if they came to London to collect it. The way in which emancipation was carried out was one of the main causes of what became known as the Great

128

Trek, in which hundreds of Boer families crossed the Orange River to put themselves beyond British sovereignty and in so doing opened up the country and created their own republics.

Casalis landed in Table Bay on February 23, 1833, after a voyage of just over three months, and hated Cape Town on sight. It was a natural reaction; he was far from home and in an alien society. But he soon recovered in the warm summer weather surrounded by all the colour and liveliness of a multi-racial seaport where he mixed with Malays and Hottentots, English clerks and Dutch farmers, where the profusion of fruit reminded him of Provence and the Languedoc.

He and his two companions were staying with Dr Philip, the superintendent of all the London Missionary Society's stations in the colony and one of the most famous missionaries in the history of the country—he was constantly vilified for his liberal views of blacks—when they heard that their destination, an Evangelical mission station even deeper in the African interior than the Reverend Moffat's at Kuruman, had been destroyed by tribes during the *difaqane* and no longer existed. The incumbent missionaries had fallen back on Moffat's station and Casalis decided to join them there. The three of them sailed to Port Elizabeth and journeyed through the Zuurveld and the Karoo, going from one mission station to the next, until they reached the L.M.S. station at Philippolis. 'Without knowing it,' Casalis wrote, 'we had reached the place and the hour where God was about to reveal the field of labour He had destined for us.'

At Philippolis, Casalis met a coloured farmer called Adam Krotz, who had a curious tale to tell. At that time the whole of the central plateau stretching north-east from Philippolis into Natal was *terra incognita* to most cartographers. In fact a map which Casalis had bought in Paris before leaving simply described it as 'sandy and desert plains', than which nothing could be further from the truth. From time to time small parties of starving Basuto had drifted down to Philippolis and Krotz had settled some of them on his farm. When they had learnt enough Dutch to be able to communicate with him they described their country, waxing particularly eloquent about the amount of wild game to be hunted. Krotz had decided to explore it.

'While I was carrying on my hunting at a place eight days' journey from here,' he told Casalis, 'a chief sent two men to beg me to visit him. I took with me as interpreter one of the natives of the country whom I had received on my farm. He conducted me to a mountain where this chief had fixed his residence and who was, for this reason, called the Mountain Chief. His true name was Moshesh, son of Mokatchane.

'He told me that for several years past he had been the victim of incessant attacks, by which three-quarters of his subjects had been destroyed or dispersed. He had asked me there to know if I could give him any good advice, if I could show him any means of securing peace for the country. I thought at once of the missionaries; I spoke to him about Moffat and about our own men (i.e. those at Philippolis). I tried to make him understand the services which such men could render him.

'The idea of having near him permanently wise men, friends of peace, disposed to do all in their power to aid him in his distress, pleased him greatly. He wanted to have some at once. "Do you know any?" he said to me, "who would be disposed to come?" I replied that such men sometimes came our way. "Oh, I beseech you, tell the first you meet to hasten here. I will give them the best possible welcome. I will do everything they advise me to do." I promised him not to forget his prayer.

'Shortly after my return home I found that he, in doubt whether I should have the means of fulfilling my promise, had sent me two hundred cattle, in order that I might procure him in exchange at least one missionary. But they had been intercepted and captured *en route* by the Koranas.'

Krotz, who was keen on another hunting expedition, offered Casalis his services as guide. There was no question in Casalis's mind that this was a call, and he accepted it.

Instead of the ten days which the journey should have taken, they were in their wagons for three weeks as Krotz and several hunting companions made detours in search of springbok, wildebeeste and eland. Their route took them over a series of high plains that rose in steppes to the line of black mountains that was their final destination. Wherever they came in sight of a village the population fled in terror and

Casalis was later told that the hunters' guns had caused the villagers to think they were Koranas.

They reached the Caledon River in June, midwinter in these latitudes, and Casalis was immediately struck by the attributes of the first Basuto clans he met. He wrote: 'Their skin was soft, bronze rather than black in colour, their limbs robust and well-modelled. Their average height was the same as our own. We were struck by the dignity of their bearing, the grace of their movements, and the deference and cordiality which characterized their manner of address. The mantles made of the skins of animals, with which they covered their shoulders, the huts in which they lived, and the pleasure they took in anointing their limbs with oil, seemed the only things that assimilated them to the savage, such as we are accustomed to conceive him.'

As they drew nearer to Moshesh's country they found ample evidence of the *difaqane*. 'Almost everywhere were human bones,' Casalis wrote. 'In some places the number indicated battle-fields. Broken earthenware, fallen walls overgrown with brambles, the easily recognized boundaries of fields formerly cultivated, revealed to us frequently that we were on the site of a once populous village. There were still some left which were inhabited, but they were much smaller and on almost inaccessible heights.'

They sent a runner to Moshesh telling him that they were near, then they crossed the icy waters of the Caledon and made camp. The following morning they were roused by Moshesh's two sons, Letsie and Molapo, who came riding down on the camp like Assyrians. 'Entire novices in the art of riding,' wrote Casalis, 'they came down on us with a rush almost without warning, at the risk of upsetting everything. It would be impossible to imagine anything more grotesque than the aspect of these young madcaps, mounted bareback, their naked legs striking the steaming flanks of their steeds like flails. The panther (leopard) skins which floated over their shoulders did not improve them. Certainly the nude is nowhere more out of place than on horseback.'

Casalis must have been relieved to discover through Krotz's interpreter that this exuberant exhibition was no more than an expression of welcome and he was told that they were not only expected, but impatiently so. Casalis at once saddled up and with Krotz and the interpreter crossed the Phuthiatsana River and began climbing Thaba Bosiu. As they followed the narrow pathway to the summit Casalis looked up and saw a long line of people forming on the edge of the rocks above, whom he at first took to be crows. The path became too steep for horses so they dismounted and walked the remainder of the slope. The moment they reached the top there was a general rush in their direction and they were surrounded by hundreds of inquisitive Basuto.

'Suddenly,' Casalis wrote, 'a personage attired in the most fantastic fashion advanced, a long wand in his hand, growling and snapping like a dog. At his appearance everybody re-treated and fell into line, making in this way an immense semi-circle behind a man seated on a mat. "There is Moshesh," said Krotz to me. The chief bent upon me a look at once majestic and benevolent. His profile, much more aquiline than that of the generality of his subjects, his well-developed fore-head, the fullness and regularity of his features, his eyes, a little weary, as it seemed, but full of intelligence and softness, made a deep impression on me. I felt at once that I had to do with a superior man, trained to think, to command others, and above all himself.

'He appeared to be about forty-five years of age. (He was, in fact, forty-seven.) The upper part of his body, entirely naked, was perfectly modelled, sufficiently fleshy, but without obesity. I admired the graceful lines of the shoulders and the fineness of his hands. He had allowed to fall carelessly around him, from his middle, a large mantle of panther skins as lissom as the finest cloth, and the folds of which covered his knees and his feet. For sole ornament he had bound round his forehead a string of glass beads, to which was fastened a tuft of feathers, which floated behind the neck. He wore on his right arm a bracelet of ivory—an emblem of power—and some copper rings on his wrists.

'After we had looked an instant at each other in silence, he rose and said, *Lumela Lekhoa*, "Welcome, white man!" and I replied by holding out my hand to him which he took without hesitation.'

* * *

132

Like the arrival of the first Portuguese mission in the City of Congo, this one had begun auspiciously. It would seem that from the very first moment of their meeting a friendship developed between Casalis and Moshesh that was unusual for its time and place; one detects an almost paternal feeling, for Moshesh was twenty-seven years older than Casalis. Whatever the root, their relationship is like no other of the period.

Having greeted each other, Moshesh took Casalis to his principal wife, Mamohato, some distance away, and the missionary was able to inspect the village. It was nothing like the City of Congo or Abomey, but simply a mass of low thatched huts built so close to each other that the thoroughfares were no more than narrow lanes and even these were encumbered by people, for most of the work, such as the preparation and cooking of food, the making of clothing, and the repair of arms, was done outside in fine weather. In the middle of the village was a huge cattle kraal, rather like a medieval bailey, where the herds were penned at night for safety. They paused at the doorway of Moshesh's main house. 'Before entering it,' Casalis wrote, 'he caused to pass before me his inferior wives, to the number of thirty or forty, not suspecting, poor man, what I thought of polygamy, nor the blows I was meditating against it.' In Mamohato's hut Casalis was given a pot of milk and what he described as a loaf of *sorgho* (sorghum) of the size and form of a cannon ball.' He sat looking helplessly at the food until one of the servants, more observant than the rest, hurried off and found him a spoon made of horn.

While he ate, he studied Moshesh's queen. She was, he says, of a somewhat ripe age, but not unattractive. She watched him with an expression that 'seemed to say that she found me very young, and that she was happy to mother me a little'. While Moshesh played with one of his young sons, Casalis finished his meal. Soon Krotz came to collect him and they descended the hill and rejoined the others at its foot. It had turned bitterly cold, which came as a shock to Casalis, who had only experienced hot weather until then, and it began to snow.

In spite of the weather, Moshesh followed them down to inspect their tents and gear and one has the impression that, just as he had shrewdly summed up what he needed from the Koranas, he was now, at the beginning of his relationship with white men, judging their culture and technology from the artefacts they had brought with them: it is a keynote of Moshesh's character that he was always willing to learn. The following evening the missionaries invited him to dinner. None had any idea of cooking and the King ended up with hashed mutton and pumpkin served on a saucepan lid. He did not mind—the mission in Paris was later to be shocked at this lack of respect—being much taken instead with a sweet white sand called sugar. The others ate directly from the saucepan itself since their plates had not been unpacked. The easy informality of the relationship between Moshesh and the missionaries is striking compared with that of the court in Dahomey and Congo. By the time the evening ended, Moshesh had invited them to remain in his country and had offered to help them get started. In return they were to pass on their knowledge to his people. A week or two later, after surveying much of the surrounding countryside, the three missionaries decided to settle in a valley they called Moriah, which is now known as Morija. It was a fair distance from Thaba Bosiu—about twenty miles—but seemed to contain everything they needed: water, wood for building and firing—lack of wood was the main reason they had not settled closer—and fertile land for growing the seeds they had brought with them.

3

A T THIS time Lesotho was untainted by any contact with outside civilization and was in that sense like the Old Kingdom before Cão's arrival. But the Basuto were an even simpler people. There was no palm-tree culture, for instance, and no coinage. Their economy was based upon cattle, the raiding of which from other clans and tribes formed their main preoccupation. Cattle were woven into the very fabric of Basuto society.

By comparison with many tribes the laws which governed them seem far from harsh and many have a Solomon-like ring. Every man was responsible for the good behaviour of his

Moshesh in 1833, just before the Boers and the British began to exert pressure on him.

Joseph Orpen

Eugene Casalis

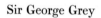
Sir George Grey

President Boshoff

Sir George Cathcart

Sir Harry Smith

Adam Kok

President Hoffman

Thaba Bosiu, the Mountain of Night, which saved the Basutos from defeat on several occasions.

Moshesh and his advisers in 1860. The man with his hand on the king's shoulder is his brother, Mopedi.

neighbour and he was liable to be punished for a crime committed by his neighbour if he failed to report it to the chief. A father was responsible for all the members of his family until they married. A village was collectively responsible for each of its inhabitants. If the skin of a stolen animal was found in a village, or the spoor traced to it, and the thief not caught, the village had to compensate the owner. This attempt to make everyone share in the responsibility of keeping the society stable is clearly shown by another law which stated that if a man saw two others fighting and made no attempt to stop them he was held jointly culpable if either was hurt.

Their sexual customs naturally seemed permissive to a succession of missionaries—who tried to change them. For example, any man who seduced or tried to seduce an unmarried girl had to pay two head of cattle; if she became pregnant, six head. Adultery, which was punished by death in some other tribes, drew a fine of two or three cows from the guilty male, also a fine of one cow from the woman's family. Meddling with a chief's wives was much more serious and anyone seducing his principal wife was either driven from the community or strangled.

The death penalty was used sparingly. Ellenberger says that the 'national sense' was always against it. This may have led to a freer society compared with many other African peoples and it is possible that the tolerance of the Basuto allowed Moshesh room for manoeuvre in his later dealings with his white neighbours, unlike the kings of Dahomey, who were caught in the chains of rigid conservatism and were unable to change even though they may have wished it, without the fear of disrupting their society.

It must be remembered that Ellenberger was a missionary and missionaries are never the most reliable judges of sexual matters. Casalis does not even comment on sexual customs. In his anthropological study of the Basuto, Hugh Ashton says that according to information he collected in the 1930s and 1940s relations between boys and girls in the old days used to be entirely innocent. So pure were the youths and maidens that they even bathed naked together and yet remained chaste. Ashton said, 'It is difficult to say how true these reports really are, and one is tempted to discount them against the familiar "things-are-not-what-they-were-when-I-was-a-child" attitude of older people. But there is no reason to suppose, as is so often done in South Africa, that Africans are "naturally" immoral and promiscuous and that therefore such chastity was improbable if not impossible.

'The general attitude still is that boys and girls and unmarried young men and especially women, should be chaste, and this is still strong enough to cause considerable individual variation. Many do keep chaste and a doctor of many years' gynaecological experience considers that an appreciable proportion of unmarried girls are virgins. On the other hand, many Basuto allege and deplore that nearly everyone has premarital love affairs: there is good evidence that some children's sexual experience begins even before puberty.'

From the first the Basuto seem to have been agriculturists, herdsmen and hunters. They had rudimentary farm implements and men, women and children worked in the fields. The men built the huts, which were made of thatching grass, and they were also the tailors, shoemakers, dressmakers, woodcarvers and implement makers. They were able to work in metal and made wood axes and battle axes, assegais and knives. The women prepared and cooked the food, were able to make and bake pottery in open-air fires of dried cow-dung, a very skilled occupation, wove sleeping mats of rushes and in general managed the house and children. They made fire by rubbing hard wood on soft and lamps by using a small pot filled with fat containing a fragment of charcoal.

Their food was plain but wholesome. They ate a porridge of ground maize or kaffir corn boiled in water, pumpkins, beans and sugar cane; bread was made from kaffir corn and they grilled meat over open fires. One of their main staples was thick milk which was kept in skins until it curdled. They made beer from the local corn. This simple diet and open air life resulted in people reaching great ages and old folk of 100 or 120 years were said not to be uncommon. They had no written language but loved to spend time listening to and telling stories, posing riddles, inventing aphorisms and proverbs, and listening to the panegyrics of their bards which told of great deeds in hunting and war.

They sound very much like 'noble savages'. And after listing some of their virtues such as energy, resolution, enterprise, cheerfulness, frankness, kindness, etc., Ellenberger turns them into human beings with the sentence, 'But they had their bad qualities as well.' And we find that they were often selfish and jealous, were given to lying and cheating, frequently stole things and enjoyed illicit sex—which went to show that they were no better and no worse than anyone else.

4

IT TOOK Casalis, Arbousset and Gossellin almost three years to settle into their new life and although Casalis put a brave face on things in his books, it is not difficult to read between the lines. At times he suffered terribly from loneliness and a mind-sapping *ennui* which he considered the particular burden of Frenchmen who are transported to alien lands. At times he was on the edge of suicide, at others, the celibacy he was forced to endure seemed to have a deleterious effect on him.

Three days after they had decided to make Moriah their base, Krotz and his hunters began the long trek back to Philippolis and, with only a tent, a wagon and a few belongings, Casalis and his friends were left utterly alone in so wild a landscape that not even the great herds of antelope appeared to have seen human beings before. 'They did not seem to trouble themselves about our presence,' Casalis wrote.

They started by building a rough cabin of tree-trunks comprising three small rooms, one in front which served as a sitting-room, a second which was the bedroom and a third in which they kept their equipment. There were no proper windows or doors but they left a few holes which allowed enough light to read by day and which at night they stuffed up with clothing. They killed a sheep or antelope once a week and hung its carcass from one of the roof-beams. It was an uncomfortable house but it only took a week to build and was not meant to be more than a stop-gap until Gossellin built their permanent home of stone.

Six weeks later Casalis made the long journey to Philippolis to buy tools and livestock. He also brought back slips of peach, apricot, fig, apple and quince trees. He bought a herd of heifers at seventeen shillings and sixpence a head, sheep at three shillings and several horses. Like all true Frenchmen, he suffered agonies because they had no flour for bread, so he brought back wheat as well as vegetable seed and potatoes. It was a hazardous journey. The country was infested with lions, but he reached Moriah in safety. A small colony had grown up around the cabin. Moshesh's son, Molapo, and a group of young men had built grass huts near by and were, on the King's orders, to help the missionaries start their farm.

Soon Casalis settled into the routine of building. 'The labours of the first three years were extremely fatiguing,' he wrote. 'The hardest came first; those demanded by the preparation of materials of construction. During entire months we were doing nothing except hewing stones, working lumps of clay for bricks, with our trousers turned up to the knees, cutting down trees and sawing them into beams and planks. Of all our work nothing was so trying as this last. ... At times one might have seen us all three stretched on our backs, exhausted, quite out of breath. ... The natives would look at us with open mouths, seeking vainly to comprehend the view of life which could lead men to kill themselves to provide so simple an affair as a shelter from the sun and rain.'

Although they were cut off from the society of other white people by the vast distances, they managed to send and receive letters, in spite of the fact that the nearest post office was at Graaff-Reinet, about three hundred miles away. Almost a year passed before they received letters written by their parents just after they had left France. Post would simply lie in Graaff-Reinet until a traveller, black or white, was going in their direction. No letters were ever lost. Later the missionaries were able to organize a postal route which speeded things up slightly; a reply from Europe now only took an average of ten months to reach them. 'In such conditions,' Casalis wrote, 'correspondence is a trial rather than a consolation.'

This feeling of bereftness, of being cut off in the midst of southern Africa, began to get him down. He started 'in [his] secret heart to nourish the unworthy hope that my life would not be a long one'. To make matters worse, he received news that his father had died. 'In the first burst of my grief there

138

was mingled a feeling akin to remorse. It was this element which gave it its bitterest pang. I seemed to myself to have killed my father.'

He was lucky that Gossellin was a practical man not given to fancies. One evening as they were seated outside the cabin, Gossellin pointed out a strip of turf under some young olive trees and offered to dig one shovelful of earth from it each day. When Casalis asked the reason Gossellin replied, 'When the hole is finished you will be just ready to be put into it!' He continued, 'Family affection is no longer a benediction when it unmans the heart, instead of fortifying it. You, so young, and yet to be thinking of ending. Why, we haven't begun yet!' Casalis said that these words were just enough to make him pull himself together.

His father's death proved to him that they were no longer regarded as strangers, for when the news got about people arrived from all sides. Moshesh sent a deputation to offer his sympathy and Casalis broke down. When he recovered he told them that his father had gone to Heaven. This confounded them for, according to their beliefs, the dead travelled in the opposite direction, sinking into the bowels of the earth.

The bereavement also had the effect of convincing the Basuto that the missionaries were not simply going to disappear one day. They had fully expected Casalis to return to France to take possession of property which they felt his father must have left him. Once they realized that the missionaries were a permanent fixture, more and more Basuto began to build huts near by and soon, under the command of another of Moshesh's sons, Letsie, there was a community of between three and four hundred people

* * *

The stone house at Moriah began to take shape; vegetables grew, and so did wheat; the fruit trees put on leaf. Slowly the mission was coming to grips with the country and the people and more time could be given to the original reason for coming to Africa. The missionaries realized that twenty miles from Thaba Bosiu was too great a distance and decided that someone must settle there if the mission was to be a success. Casalis volunteered. But the stock of furniture and utensils was only sufficient for the mission house so once more he had to make the long journey into the Cape Colony and back again. When he came to leave Moriah there were touching scenes, for although he would not be going far, the missionaries knew they would seldom see each other. Gossellin came with Casalis to help build a small shack on a hillock below Thaba Bosiu, then he returned to Moriah.

'Then commenced for me,' Casalis wrote, 'a kind of life which was the quintessence of all the difficulties and all the vexations which I had known up to then, but of which I had before borne only a third. *Vae soli*! "Woe to the solitary!" I experienced in its every phase, from the time of my waking till the hour of sleep, and during the watches of the night, the terrible truth of that word.' He tried to counteract his loneliness by work; he started a small school, he visited the huts, he preached, he helped to improve agriculture, he advised on the construction of bigger dwellings. But gradually the panacea itself began to overwhelm him. 'When was I to find time for it,' he wrote, 'obliged as I was to prepare as well as I could, my own meals, repair my clothes and linen, and keep up a measure of order and decency about me?'

He spent a great deal of time brooding about this question and realized that if he had no help he could not go on. He needed a companion. Marriage! The very thought, he said, made him tremble. 'I, who was already more than half a savage . . . where and how to find the other?' But clearly the need for a wife had been in his mind for some time for he had already written to the Society in Paris as well as to his mother to get their permission. So he set off on his travels once more, this time a horse-back journey all the way to Cape Town, where he found a wife, Sarah Dyke, whom he married in April 1836, returning with her to Lesotho after two months. They spent some time at Moriah, then moved to Thaba Bosiu. Casalis's unique position among the Basuto might have suffered had they taken a dislike to his wife. As it was, he could hardly have done better. Mrs Casalis, with her blue eyes and fair skin, was at first an object of wonder, then, as she nursed the sick and worked tirelessly among children and old people she was taken into the Basuto family like her husband and given the name 'Ma-Eugene' after the birth of her first child.

These years were vital for the Basuto, in view of what was to come. It is quite possible that if Casalis had delayed going to Thaba Bosiu for a few years he might never have been allowed to settle there, for, by the 1840s, white pressure on the Kingdom was enormous and the elders of the Basuto people might well have persuaded the King not to allow white people—including the French missionaries—to settle anywhere near them. But he was in time. And although he never succeeded in making a Christian out of Moshesh, and although Moshesh did not always take his advice, Casalis's influence on the development of Lesotho was very great.

However, before these political crises followed each other, he had begun his mission work at Thaba Bosiu, actively assisted by Moshesh. Whenever he wished to preach, Moshesh ordered his public crier to call everyone together, including the women and children. The tribal elders at first did not care to be humiliated by the presence of females, but Moshesh was firm. When the women, fearful or embarrassed at what might happen, sent their children in their places, Moshesh would call out, 'Where are the women?' Then, when they had shuffled forward and squatted down in shy groups, the King would turn to Casalis, standing on a specially built platform, and say, 'They are here. Begin.'

Often at night Moshesh would invite Casalis to one of his huts where they would talk. Sometimes the King's advisers would be there as well and they would discuss their different ideas of the world, humanity and the Creation. One night Casalis promulgated the doctrinal thesis that God created Man of one blood.

'What?' cried one of the tribal elders. 'That can never be. You are white; we are black: how could we come from the same father?' Moshesh turned on him, pointing out that in his herds there were white, red and spotted cattle. Did they not all come from the same stock and belong to the same master? On another occasion when Moshesh was discussing his basic belief in the unity of mankind he made one of those remarks that come ringing down the years. 'Black or white,' he said, 'we laugh or cry in the same manner; what gives pleasure or pain to the one race, causes equally pleasure or pain to the other.'

141

A great friendship grew up over the years between the two men and Casalis became one of the most powerful figures in the Kingdom. Moshesh called him 'my white man' and would send for him at any time to ask his advice or just to chat. The King seems to have been something of an insomniac for he would often take Casalis into an empty hut at night and they would talk for hours on end, sometimes until the first rays of dawn. He would then rise, go to the door of the hut, call out, 'Ah! Dia ha!' ('I have seen the light'), and return to his hut and go to sleep, leaving Casalis to go wearily off about his business. Casalis was told that this unfailing cry of joy at the first hint of dawn was a daily reminder to Moshesh of the time when, hemmed in by enemies, he went to sleep each night with the thought that he would be killed before morning.

The most serious division between the two was over the vexed question of polygamy and Casalis chipped away at the King over the years, without success. 'The subject often came up in our conversations. We (the missionaries) never introduced it in a special or direct manner in our preaching because we well knew that a reformation in this matter could only be the natural and spontaneous fruit of a cordial adoption of the great Christian principle. But Moshesh made no difficulty about discussing it with us.

'"You are right", he would say. "Even with us there have been, in all time, men here and there who were content with one wife, and, far from blaming them, they have always been cited as models. Since we do not admit that one woman has the right to several husbands, one does not see why a man should have the right to several wives. And then if you knew what these women make us suffer by their quarrels, and the rivalry which they foment amongst our children! . . . With all my herds and my stocks of grain, there are days when I am in danger of dying of hunger because all my wives are sulking with me, sending me from one to the other. . . . Our women age quickly, and then we cannot resist the temptation of taking younger ones. Amongst the older women there are some who become idle and they are the first to advise us to take another wife, hoping to make a servant of her."'

Moshesh described polygamy as a strong citadel and feared

that neither Casalis nor his colleagues would be able to shake it, and he pointed out that it took a long time to get white people to content themselves with one wife. 'We will talk of this again,' he would say, leaving the subject wide open. 'It is certainly annoying there should be this difference between you and us. Without that we should soon be Christians.'

5

WHILE MOSHESH was testing his dialectic in these sessions with Casalis, and while the mission at Moriah was gradually expanding and extending its influence, things were happening beyond the encircling mountains that were going to have a profound effect on Lesotho; it was about to be dragged, however unwillingly, into the arena of white power politics. As scheduled, the slaves had been freed and as foreseen the way it had been done had caused widespread dissatisfaction, setting off the Great Trek.

In 1836 hundreds of farmers of Dutch and French extraction left British authority and crossed the Orange River into what they considered was no-man's-land and is now known as the Orange Free State, Natal and the Transvaal; some pressed farther and farther into the interior, others decided to settle as soon as they were beyond British jurisdiction. However, under a scheme put forward by Dr Philip, Casalis's friend and mentor at the Cape, the Cape Colony was now ringed by statelets ruled by the Griqua chiefs Adam Kok and Andries Waterboer, and a third by Moshesh. When the Griquas tried to enforce their rule on the trekkers they were ignored. But Moshesh could not be ignored. In the early 1840s his tribe was estimated to be between thirty and forty thousand strong; he had the ear and the sympathy of his missionaries—more stations had been founded by both French and Wesleyan missions—and he watched the settlement of farmers near his borders with displeasure; he himself was planning to expand his territory and increase the size of his nation.

Events to the north and north-east of him had conspired to make this dream a possibility. Moselekatze and his Matabele had been defeated by the Boer trekkers and driven

143

across the Limpopo River into what is now Rhodesia and, closer to home, Dingane, Shaka's heir, was defeated by the Boers at Blood River. All the shattered tribes which had been living from hand to mouth since the *difaqane* now came out into the sun once more. From his eyrie in fortress-Lesotho, Moshesh watched this particular change thoughtfully. The two most powerful black leaders in southern Africa had been eliminated and he had the whole field to himself. The historian George McCall Theal, who had no love for blacks, wrote, 'This is crediting him [Moshesh] with powers of observation greater than those of all the officers of the Colonial Government and of all the missionaries with the different tribes. But it is no more than his due. For ages the Bantu have been developing this peculiar kind of intelligence, and Moshesh was the cleverest man that the race has produced in modern times.'

His general unease at the arrival near him of white trekkers was intensified by several incidents, two of which left lasting impressions. In the first, one of the trek leaders, Piet Retief, managed by trickery to handcuff Sikonyela, now chief of the Batlokwa. He was told he would only be released when disputed cattle were returned. That a chief could be so treated had a great effect on the Basuto and in the future it provided Moshesh with an excuse on several occasions not to meet white officials. When he did meet them he almost always insisted that Casalis or another of the missionaries go with him.

The second incident concerned one of the ablest of the trekker leaders, Andries Willem Pretorius, who tried and executed an envoy from Dingane. This act, which Theal describes as 'a great mistake and a great crime', horrified the Basuto even more. It was one of their most sacred laws that an ambassador was sacrosanct. Casalis quoted this in his book, *The Basutos*: 'The person of a messenger is inviolable. This principle has passed into a proverb: *Lengosa ga le molatu* (a delegate can have no fault).' What particularly appalled the Basuto was that the whites were Christians yet they respected neither the person of a chief nor the life of a chief's messenger.

Much of the history of South Africa is the story of boundary and border disputes, from the time of the first settlement when the Hottentots, the original people of the Cape of Good

144

Hope, found themselves excluded from certain areas by decree of the Dutch East India Company, to the mid-nineteenth century when there were constant border disputes between Bantu and British, Bantu and Boer, Bantu and Bantu, and British and Boer. A series of Xhosa wars was fought on the eastern frontier in which the names of boundary rivers —the Kei, the Keiskama, the Great Fish, the Sundays—pass like signposts in a colonial nightmare. The history of these border disputes, and their manifold results, is so complex as to make even the most political of historians blench.

What happened is what had already happened in the Old Kingdom of Congo and in every other black kingdom where whites had arrived; two irreconcilable philosophies had met head on: the black and white conception of land-holding. As has already been said, the black view was that the land belonged in perpetuity to the tribe which held it, it was indivisible. This clashed violently with the white philosophy of private ownership and the sanctity of property. What made it worse was that while the whites wanted everything down on paper, exact definitions, exact boundaries, the black kings consciously tended to leave them vague.

By the beginning of the 1840s things were building up to the first disputes between Moshesh and the Boers who had settled along the lower Caledon River. Some were beyond even the most shadowy of his boundaries; others were well within. At the beginning they were received by Moshesh on terms of friendship and allowed to build houses, plant crops and graze cattle. It was a vast, underpopulated landscape and there was plenty of room for everyone. But the Boers were 'settlers'. The very act of building a house and planting crops meant they were staking their claim to the land, they were putting down roots. In Moshesh's view they were simply occupying the land at his pleasure; neither he nor anyone else could divide it up for private ownership. It was not long before cattle thefts began to disrupt the early harmony. The same thing was happening in the two Griqua states but on a much greater scale. However, most of the Griqua clans were under the protection of the powerful London Missionary Society. The Society put pressure on the British Government and Britain warned the emigrant farmers not to interfere with the Griquas or the Basutos. This meant that the Boers had no rights of protection in these territories, something that added fuel to the anti-British feeling many of them had nurtured since birth.

In 1843 Moshesh signed a treaty with Britain by which he was to receive £75 a year either in money or arms, in return for holding his part of the frontier of the Cape Colony against all comers; to surrender all criminals and fugitives; and generally to act as an ally of the Cape Administration. The treaty also made an attempt at defining what these borders were but since they had been neither surveyed nor discussed Moshesh was placed, for an annual pittance, in a difficult situation. There were immediate protests by the Wesleyan missionaries at Thaba Nchu who suddenly found themselves part of Moshesh's territory when they had considered the huge tracts of land surrounding their mission to be held by them on behalf of their Baralong and Griqua flocks. Letters of protest and explanation began to fly between the Cape Government and the Orange River area.

Beyond Moshesh's boundaries, tension was growing between the Boers and Adam Kok's Griquas. There were disputes, then incidents. A Boer force took the field, a British flying column raced up from the Cape and dispersed it. This column, small though it was, had a great influence on Moshesh. It consisted of two squadrons of the 7th Dragoon Guards wearing brass helmets and red coats and carrying rifles as well as the traditional swords; two guns, six-pounders of the Royal Artillery; two companies of the 91st Regiment (1st Battalion of the Argyll and Sutherland Highlanders), and two troops of the Cape Mounted Rifles, which was a mixed force of whites and Hottentots. All the men were well-armed and well-mounted and the sight of them reinforced Moshesh's early decision to concentrate on cavalry and guns in his own army.

Speeches were made, a shaky peace established, boundaries were marked and a small detachment of fifty-eight troopers under Captain (late Major) Warden were left to keep the peace in an area of about fifty thousand square miles. Encroachment continued, so did cattle-reiving by both white and black, with the resulting recovery raids. The country was in an uproar. On the Cape Colony's eastern border, British troops

146

were engaged in a seemingly never-ending series of wars, the Kaffir Wars, with Bantu tribes. In the midst of this Moshesh was expected, without help, to maintain his boundaries and keep his country stable.

It was at this point that a new figure entered the history of Lesotho. He was Sir Harry Smith, a soldier's soldier who exploded on to the veld like a firecracker. He gave the impression of never being still, never weary, always in motion. Major-General Sir Harry George Wakelyn Smith, to give him his full title, was born in 1787 and by the time he entered Moshesh's life had served in South America, had fought in the Peninsular War and at Waterloo, and had earned the title, the 'Victor of Aliwal' after his famous victory in 1846 when he defeated a Sikh army at the village of Aliwal in the Punjab. A portrait of him painted in 1856 when he was sixty-nine shows a man still young-looking for his years, with the face of a country squire who might have been found galloping through the pages of Surtees. There is also a look of the Duke of Wellington about him, big-nosed and long-faced.

As a dashing young captain, he had been at the siege of Badajoz in Spain in 1812. When the town fell, British troops ran amok. In his book, *The Age of Elegance*, Sir Arthur Bryant described what happened:

'The men, separated in the darkness from their officers, parched with thirst and half-mad from the fury of the attack, broke into the cellars and wineshops. By dawn they had become a mob of fiends. They had been promised, in accordance with the rules of war, that if the garrison resisted after the breaches had been made, the city would be given up to sack . . . Women were dragged screaming from hiding holes and raped, wine casks were broached in the streets, and satyrs with blackened faces drank till the liquor ran from their mouths and ears. No officer could control them . . .

'Down at the camp below the town, where the British wounded lay in thousands, two young officers, standing at their tent door on the day after the attack, saw two Spanish ladies approaching, the elder of whom, her ears torn and bleeding from the grasp of drunken savages, confided to their protection her sister, a girl of fifteen. Such was her faith in the British character, she declared, that she knew the appeal

147

would not be in vain. "Nor was it", wrote one of the officers. "Nor could it be abused for she stood by the side of an angel— a being more transcendently lovely than any I had ever before beheld. To look at her was to love her—and I did love her, but I never told her my love, and in the meantime another and a more impudent fellow stepped in and won her!" Two days later Juanita Maria de los Dolores de Leon was married to Captain Harry Smith of the Rifles. The Commander-in-Chief gave her away, and she became the darling of the Army, henceforward sharing all its adventures and hardships. Many years later, when her husband, the Victor of Aliwal, had become the hero of Victorian England and Governor of the Cape, she gave her name to a South African town destined to become the scene of another famous siege.' This was Ladysmith which was besieged for 130 days in the Boer War.

Sir Harry was just the sort of person the Cape colonists loved: he had fought in the war of 1835 and now, at sixty, he was back in the country as Governor and High Commissioner, having gone on record as guaranteeing he would finish any future Kaffir War in three weeks at the most. Unhappily, while he knew the old trade of warfare, he knew little or nothing about civil administration. That did not deter him. In January, 1848, he rode north with only his personal staff to see what chance there was of bringing the trekkers back into the British fold. It was plain there was none. So instead he proclaimed 'the Sovereignty of Her Majesty the Queen of England over the Territories north of the Great Orange River, including the countries of Moshesh, Moroko, Moletsane, Sikonyela, Adam Kok, Gert Taaibosch, and other minor chiefs as far north as the Vaal River, and east to the Drakensberg . . .' This meant that the trekkers had to become British subjects or move on once again. And, while Sir Harry disclaimed any intention of increasing British territory, his proclamation was, in effect, one of the largest annexations in South African history.

The declaration of the Sovereignty was made in the small trekker village of Winburg in February. Moshesh was there, so was Casalis. Casalis wrote: 'His Excellency [Smith] was very gracious, spoke to me in French (very well); recalled the Pyrénées and the Battle of Orthez, at which he had been

148

present; complimented Moshesh on his skill in horsemanship; told him that he knew him well, and had often heard him spoken of; made him a present of two new saddles of the latest make, of a marquee tent, a gold watch (all this whilst cantering for half an hour); asked him if the country of Winburg belonged to the Basutos to which Moshesh replied in the affirmative ... We entered the village under a fire of musketry.' Sir Harry told Moshesh that although the muskets made the sound of war they were being used now as a sign of peace to which Moshesh replied in his most pious voice, 'Peace is the mother of nations.' They spent some time talking together in Sir Harry's tent and Moshesh mentioned the disputes existing between himself and several other chiefs including Sikonyela and Moroko. 'Trust me,' said Sir Harry, 'and no one will dare to raise his hand against the Great Chief of the Basutos.' Then, according to Casalis, he raised his right hand about a foot above the desk and said, 'Moshesh is like this.' Then, raising his left hand another foot above the right he said, 'But Her Majesty is as this! . . .'

Soon afterwards he called a meeting with the Boers and presented Moshesh to them. Holding him by the hand he told them they were indebted to Moshesh for the peace they had enjoyed. He said: 'Let no man move from his place on which he is, and let no man presume to encroach upon Moshesh.' If they spoke of revolt and were determined to recommence their oppressions in other parts he, the Governor, would 'follow them' up, even though it were to the gates of the infernal regions!

Before Sir Harry dashed back to the Cape, he and Moshesh exchanged letters denouncing the farmers. They were published and gave the trekkers further cause for disenchantment. A bare six months later, the farmers were once more in arms, this time having called on their compatriots north of the Vaal to come to their aid. Major Warden and his small body of men were no match for them. The Boer leader Pretorius forced him to cross the Orange River under a safe conduct but not before Warden had sent a letter to Moshesh apprising him of the situation. Moshesh had been waiting for what he called the fight between the two 'white bulls' and he now lay low, watching and waiting. Sir Harry, on the other hand, went off like a rocket. On July 29 he and his staff left Cape Town in three horse-drawn wagons and, travelling at six miles an hour, they reached Colesberg, 615 miles to the north, on August 9. By the 27th he and his mixed force of regulars and Griquas numbering about five hundred was across the Orange River and marching towards Bloemfontein. The two forces met at Boomplaats, and Sir Harry won an easy victory. Once again he disappeared south, leaving Warden and his small force to rule the Sovereignty.

Moshesh had been watching the events with troubled interest and drew two conclusions: he was certain now that of the opposing white races the most powerful, and therefore the one with which he would side, was the British. But they had a habit of vanishing south leaving him to defend his own lands, so it seemed only prudent to increase his strength as much as he could. The Basuto were ordered to find horses and guns any way they could; by working for white farmers or by stealing them if necessary. Gun-running had started on the borders of the black states and the Basuto welcomed unscrupulous white dealers. Since the Napoleonic wars, most of the world's active armies had been re-armed with percussion-lock muskets and there were hundreds of thousands of obsolete flintlocks lying about the Continent and Britain. A fair proportion found their way into Lesotho in exchange for cattle, and in a few years Moshesh was able to field a force of about seven thousand men, well-mounted and adequately armed.

6

'FOR SOME years,' Casalis wrote, 'the incessant pressure of the whites appears to have opened the eyes of the natives: their attention was more drawn to whatever affected their common interests: the chiefs became more indispensable to their subjects and the idea of a general confederation of the tribes formed for the purpose of making headway against a foreign race seemed to grow every day.'[1]

[1] This vital passage, as Tylden points out, appears only in the original French version of Les Bassoutos and was never, for some reason, translated.

It is likely that the growing unease among the tribes was the start of an anti-white feeling. Tylden wrote: 'However much Moshesh might profit by his association with white people, and there is no doubt he did profit and fully realized it, there was much to cause him serious uneasiness. As time went on that uneasiness grew.' What particularly worried him was the off-hand manner and lack of dignity with which the British had been treating tribal chiefs who expected and received immense respect not only from their own people but from all other tribes. Moshesh's network of messengers going backwards and forwards across the Drakensberg into Natal and the Eastern Cape brought him similar stories from all parts of the country. Nor could he understand how the British (i.e. white people) could take the side of groups of Hottentots, whom Moshesh considered treacherous, against the trekkers, who were also white. Another difficulty for Moshesh was the religion which Casalis and Arbousset had brought to his country. They had preached peace on earth. Yet he had only to look around him to see that all the whites were at least as warlike as the Bantu themselves. Moshesh's fertile mind evolved a philosophy to capitalize on the situation. In general he wanted a confederation of black tribes to counteract white pressure and, in particular, as a backstop, so to speak, in case this did not work, an alliance with Britain. But the alliance was proving difficult because of the Basutos' desire to run with the hare and hunt with the hounds. While proclaiming friendship with Britain, they, at the same time, ignored Warden and his boundary—the Warden Line—between Boer and Basuto and continued their depredations in the Sovereignty. Indeed, two of Moshesh's sons, Letsie and Nehemiah, who had been educated at the Cape, returned to Lesotho and immediately began raiding cattle. In one raid against Sikonyela, the Basutos, according to Major Warden, lifted 73 horses, 6,303 cattle, 2,470 sheep and 2,966 goats. They did so with Moshesh's connivance, for cattle-raiding was in the direct Basuto tradition of proving one's manhood; it was the way Moshesh had proved his own, the way he had gathered his power. Complaints reached Warden, who wrote to Sir Harry.

'It is evident to me,' Sir Harry replied, 'that Moshesh is acting dishonestly and that the ambition of his sons has prompted him to the improper line he has pursued. Your suggestion therefore that this Chief must be humbled . . . must be carried out . . . If Moshesh shuts himself up in his mountain . . . I believe some howitzer shells may be thrown upon him . . .' Sir Godfrey Lagden, who was High Commissioner in Lesotho later on, says in his book, *The Basutos*, 'In these words are to be read the first rumblings of the wars to follow later. Sir Harry Smith had clearly flung away the scabbard.'

Moshesh quickly became the focus of Major Warden's displeasure. After a Basuto attack on Chief Moroko near Thaba Nchu, Warden wrote to Sir Harry, 'The Basuto people are proud and insolent towards their neighbours . . . the time is not distant, I imagine, when it will be necessary to place them under restraint. . . . The Basuto require humbling . . .' To Moshesh Warden wrote, 'Depend upon it that however strong you may imagine yourself to be, there is a stronger hand ready to punish the wicked doings of a people ten times more powerful than the Basuto.' Moshesh ignored him and during the months that followed the cattle raiding increased. Warden became more and more angry, and it is easy to see why. He had an impossible job trying to police an area of fifty thousand square miles where the blacks and half-castes were natural cattle-reivers, the whites were natural land-grabbers and Moshesh, sitting like some great spider in his web of mountains, must have seemed the worst of all with his pious replies to letters of accusation, his clever French missionaries, his reluctance to come off his mountain for meetings and his willingness to sign papers agreeing to boundaries he had no intention of keeping. In June, 1851, Warden wrote to him demanding six thousand 'good cattle' and three hundred horses in fines and reparations. He ordered them to be delivered within ten days—an impossible demand. By the time Moshesh received the letter a mixed force of about a thousand comprising, British, Griquas, Baralongs and some Boers who did not mind in whose company they fought as long as it was against Moshesh, was perched on his borders. Warden had had enough. 'Prosecute the war . . .' Sir Harry had written, and this he was doing. But Moshesh had long been prepared for such a contingency.

When the combined column advanced they were attacked by a vassal tribe of the Basutos, the Bataung, from the steep-sided heights of Viervoot Hill. Warden ordered Major Donovan, who had command of the troops, to storm the heights. But neither of the two six-pounder guns could be man-handled up the seven-hundred-foot slopes. The British and Boers halted at the top. The Baralong advanced, chasing away a few Bataung cattle guards and reached the nearest village. There they found beer. In a short time most were too drunk to fight. The battle had begun at seven in the morning, by eleven the Basuto force arrived. One of the guns was nearly captured and was hastily withdrawn. The Boers were set the task of trying to extricate the Baralong. By mid-afternoon the combined force, which had lost 152 killed, was in retreat. The humiliation was completed and the Sovereignty lay open to whatever Moshesh might do against it.[1]

Here again he showed his diplomatic skill. He made no move; he had previously warned the farmers not to join Warden's force—most had not served—and he now contented himself with minor raids on those who had been unwise enough to fight him.

The battle of Viervoot had widespread repercussions. The French missionaries wrote a memorial to the British Government in which they not only gave an eye-witness account of the fight but the reasons leading up to it. 'We think', they wrote, 'there has been an unwarrantable disregard of the rights, the past history, the different habits, the relative position and the respective wants of the native population. This had led the natives to suspect the Government of a disposition to *divide in order to reign* ... Natural rights, past grievances, past benefits, past engagements and treaties, feudal allegiances, kindred ties, family bonds, have been discarded and overlooked.

'Moshesh has been placed on a level with chieftains whom he had received in the land ... This astounding mode of

[1] Curiously enough, a black writer, S. M. Molema, gives a different outcome. In his book, *The Basuto Past and Present*, published in 1920, he wrote, 'In the interests of the Orange Free State they [the British] reinforced by the Thaba Ncho Baralongs *attacked* [his italics] Moshesh and defeated him at Vierfirt [*sic*].'

government has been crowned by employing one tribe against another ... A chief who would have had no objection to meeting the British Resident (Warden) personally is filled with indignation by the prospect of finding himself surrounded by men with whom he has been at war in bygone days and who are ready to exult in his humiliation ... Limits have been made in the very centre of the territory of Moshesh (the Batlokwa had been settled nearer him) contrary to the solemn promises made to him in conferences with the highest English authorities ... nothing less than the prospect of irretrievable ruin could prompt us to speak as we do this day. The perversion of the feelings of the people is already frightful. War will drive them completely back to barbarism. No resource remains to them if vanquished than to take refuge in the recesses and strongholds of their mountains. This once accomplished, it may be safely predicted, that the Sovereignty will be untenable for civilized men during many years.'

The memorial was undoubtedly partial but its weight, coming on top of pressure by the London Missionary Society, made an impression on the British Government, and the Colonial Secretary, Lord Grey, wrote that 'the ultimate abandonment of the Orange Sovereignty should be a settled point in our policy'. The British Government had never wanted the Sovereignty, indeed, they did not even want South Africa, except for the Cape Peninsula as a revictualling stop on the voyage to India. 'They were weary of kaffir wars,' wrote the historian Eric A. Walker, 'which only seemed to benefit land speculators and shop-keepers who naturally liked a large garrison; the Sovereignty was worthless in their eyes ...'

There was a flurry of activity: Sir Harry Smith was recalled; a two-man commission, Major Hogge and Mr Owen, was sent to the Sovereignty and signed the Sand River Convention with the Boers declaring that Britain had no interest in and would not attempt to rule the land across the Vaal River. This meant a further exodus of farmers away from the Sovereignty, away from British rule, to the present Transvaal. In the Sovereignty the commissioners dismissed a few officials, and condemned the Warden Line as unjust to the Basutos, but demanded huge reparations from Moshesh for earlier crimes. Warden himself was replaced.

154

But nothing changed. The cattle-raiding by both sides on the border grew worse. Something final had to be done to bring about peace. A new man was sent out from Britain. He was Sir George Cathcart who replaced Sir Harry Smith. Following Smith's policy, he had ended the latest Kaffir War—which had been fought on the eastern coast of the country near the present towns of East London and King William's Town—and now he could turn his attention to the Sovereignty. In December, 1852, he mobilized 2,500 men at the village of Burgersdorp in the north-east section of the Cape Colony.

Lieutenant-General Sir George Cathcart was a very different man from Smith. Unlike Sir Harry, who always looked upon himself as a plain soldier, Cathcart was the son of an earl. During his army career he had seen service in 1813 in Germany and 1814 in France, and had become a favourite of the Duke of Wellington, whose influence had secured him the governorship of the Cape. His portrait shows a man of imperious bearing with a determined mouth but sensitive eyes. The historian Cory describes him as 'tall and slim and one of the kindest and gentlest of men'. He was predisposed in favour of the blacks—which was just as well since the British Government's policy was one of *rapprochement* with the tribes—and ended up with no great opinion of the white colonists, a feeling that was reciprocated in some quarters. He was in favour of abandoning the Sovereignty, but first he, too, considered that Moshesh needed to be taught a lesson.

'There yet remained one rankling sore to be healed before it could safely be said that all was peace and that the maintenance of a large force could safely be dispensed with,' he wrote to the British Secretary of State. 'I allude to the protracted state of petty warfare which exists in the Sovereignty between the dependents of the paramount Basuto chief, Moshesh, and a portion of the burgher (farmer) population bordering on his territory.'

And again: 'If I make war on Moshesh, it must be on good grounds and a well-established *casus belli*, and then it must be no small war.'

He also decided that he would use only regular troops and would not ask white farmers, Griquas, Koranas or Baralongs to help him. His force comprised two thousand infantry, five hundred cavalry and two guns. He thought it perfectly adequate. Now he only needed the *casus belli*. From his encampment at Burgersdorp he crossed the Orange River in very hot weather and arrived at the Wesleyan mission of Platberg a few miles north-west of Thaba Bosiu on December 13, 1852. The following day he sent a letter to Moshesh demanding, in reparation for previous raids, a total of ten thousand cattle and one thousand horses. This was somewhat less than Hogge and Owen had asked for but Cathcart demanded that they should be delivered *in three days*. The following day Moshesh arrived at the British camp with Casalis and a number of counsellors. Hundreds of Basuto who had tried to accompany him were driven back by the King with his riding-crop. Moshesh was dressed in a blue jacket, gold-laced trousers and a cap. The Governor and his staff were also splendid in gold braid and stood outside a marquee to greet Moshesh. The Basuto delegation were led to three tents where food and drink awaited them. When they had refreshed themselves the conference began, Casalis and his brother-in-law, Dyke, acting as interpreters. It was, by any standards, a remarkable confrontation and an official minute exists. After the briefest of pleasantries they got down to business.

GOVERNOR: I will not now talk much, but wish to know whether you received my message yesterday, in which I made the demand for cattle and horses. I have nothing to alter in that letter.

MOSHESH: Do you mean the letter I received from Mr Owen?

GOVERNOR: Yes.

MOSHESH: I received that letter, but do not know where I shall get the cattle from. Am I to understand that the ten thousand head demanded are a fine imposed for thefts committed by my people, in addition to the stolen cattle?

GOVERNOR: I demand but ten thousand, though your people have stolen many more, but consider this a just award, which must be paid in three days.

MOSHESH: Do the three days count from yesterday or today?

GOVERNOR: Today is the first of the three.

MOSHESH: The time is short and the cattle many. Will you not allow me six days to collect them?

GOVERNOR: You had time given you when Major Hogge and Mr Owen made the first demand and then you promised to comply with it, but did not.

MOSHESH: But I was not quite idle. Do not the papers in the Commissioner's hands show that I collected them?

GOVERNOR: They do. But not half the number.

MOSHESH: That is true, but I have not now control enough over my people to induce them to comply with the demand, however anxious I may be to do so.

GOVERNOR: If you are not able to collect them, I must go and do it; and if any resistance be made it will then be war, and I shall not be satisfied with ten thousand head, but shall take all I can.

MOSHESH: Do not talk of war, for, however anxious I may be to avoid it, you know that a dog when beaten will show his teeth.

GOVERNOR: It will therefore be better that you should give up the cattle than that I should go for them.

MOSHESH: I wish for peace; but have the same difficulty with my people that you have in the colony. Your prisons are never empty, and I have thieves among my people.

GOVERNOR: I would then recommend you to catch the thieves and bring them to me and I will hang them.

MOSHESH: I do not wish you to hang them, but to talk to them and give them advice. If you hang them, they cannot talk.

GOVERNOR: If I hang them they cannot steal, and I am not going to talk any more, I have said that if you do not give up the cattle in three days, I must come and take them.

MOSHESH: I beg of you not to talk of war.

But Cathcart had come to do nothing else, and by giving Moshesh only three days to deliver ten thousand head of cattle—an almost impossible task—he had manufactured his own *casus belli*.

The dialogue between the two men sounds neutered, set down in the formal phraseology of Government minutes. There is another source. Sergeant James McKay of the 74th

157

Regiment (2nd Battalion Highland Light Infantry) was on guard that day. He recalled heated words and fists slamming on tables, the Governor springing to his feet saying that he would give Moshesh four days to bring in the cattle and horses (this was a late concession). And then, thumping the table again to emphasize his point, 'If they don't bring them, I will go and fetch them!' And Moshesh replying strongly, 'Well, your Excellency, you know that when a dog is kicked he generally turns and bites!'

The concession of the extra day did not, in the event, matter: the Basuto were never going to hand over ten thousand cattle. But days of grace had been offered and days of grace were taken; the troops sat down to wait. Besides the Royal Artillery, the force with Cathcart consisted of two squadrons 12th Royal Lancers, two companies Cape Mounted Rifles, four companies of the 2nd Queen's (the West Surrey Regiment), three companies of the 43rd Regiment (1st Battalion the Oxford & Bucks Light Infantry) and 73rd Regiment (2nd Battalion the Black Watch), four companies 74th Regiment (2nd Battalion the Highland Light Infantry) and one company of the 1st Battalion the Rifle Brigade. The officers and men were all veterans of the Kaffir Wars on the eastern frontier of the colony. The Rifle Brigade and a few specialists in other companies carried rifles which far outranged the Basuto muskets; but the rest of the force were armed with smoothbore muskets not much better than the Basuto flintlocks. The Basuto, of course, could make no reply to the howitzers and rocket tubes.

The wait could not have been too arduous for the troops for it was typical High Veld summer weather of warm sunny days and afternoon thunderstorms which cooled the air and settled the dust. They were extremely well victualled. Their supply train comprised 164 wagons—the entire column occupied six miles on the march—and to their surprise they had been able to buy such luxuries as Crosse and Blackwell's pickles, and bottles of Bass's India Pale Ale in the village of Burgersdorp.

On December 17 Cathcart broke his resolve not to use tribesmen. He sent guns and ammunition to Sikonyela's Batlokwa, Moshesh's most uncompromising enemies, and de-

158

manded their help if there was fighting. He also called on Moroko to place his Baralongs along the road to Bloemfontein to protect his line of communication. On the 18th, Nehemiah, one of Moshesh's sons, drove three thousand five hundred head of cattle, some in poor condition, into Cathcart's camp. They were escorted by five hundred mounted men and the British troops were able to view their enemy. The Basuto were described as being well mounted, riding on primitive saddles which hurt the backs of their ponies and using leather thongs for stirrups. They carried assegais in leather quivers on their backs, held a musket in one hand and many had a light battle-axe, the national weapon, tied to the saddle. On their heads, they wore balls made of ostrich feathers, jackals' tails and wildebeeste manes. With reason, they were described as 'wild-looking'. One of the French missionaries arrived to beg for more time, but no answer was given. Early on the morning of the 20th the British force crossed the Caledon River into Lesotho; what was to become officially known as the Affair at the Berea had begun.

7

BEREA MOUNTAIN, NAMED after a mission at its base, is really a high plateau with steep sides that made ascent difficult; such flat-topped plateaux and smaller hills—Thaba Bosiu itself, for instance—are not uncommon in southern Africa and are often to be seen rising out of bare plains. The Berea lay directly between Platberg mission and Thaba Bosiu and overlooked Moshesh's stronghold. Several precipitous paths led to the top where there was excellent grazing and springs of good water, ideal pasturage, easily defended. As Cathcart approached the plateau he saw herds of cattle on the top and since the capture of cattle was one of the objects of the expedition here was an opportunity not to be missed; he decided to take the Berea.

He split his force into three divisions, one under his own command, one under Colonel Eyre, which consisted mostly of infantry, pack mules and a few rockets; and a third, the mounted men, under Colonel Napier, Cape Mounted Rifles.

The plan was that Eyre should ascend the plateau, round up the cattle, drive them down the paths and join up with Napier, who was to circle the plateau's northern end, and the Governor, who would circle it to the south, on the plain before Thaba Bosiu. Both Eyre and Napier had orders not to fire unless fired upon. But when Napier's cavalry saw the cattle they could not resist them.

Tylden described what happened next: 'There is a fairly obvious and not very steep way up, and Napier, sending a troop from each regiment as advance guard, followed them on to the tableland. There were only cattle guards in front of him and these fired from behind a stone wall and were charged and dispersed by the advance guard. The top of the Berea is rolling country with dead ground everywhere and the cavalry soon found themselves galloping in scattered formation trying to collect cattle. The cattle, excited by the herds' calling and whistling, were half frantic and in one place it was only by shooting an ox and blocking a footpath off the hill that they could be stopped. At nine a.m. Casalis and Dyke at the mission at Thaba Bosiu were watching the Lancers up on the Berea firing their pistols at the cattle herds. By midday, Napier had begun to move off down his track of the morning with four thousand head of cattle. Major Tottenham, 12th Lancers, with thirty of his regiment, was acting as rearguard, and away to his proper left nearer the Berea mission was a party of both regiments. Molapo (another of Moshesh's sons), with his own men and some Bataung, about seven hundred men in all, had come up close to the rearguard and were waiting to attack. He put in a party of footmen from the nearest villages and then moved forward. He outflanked Tottenham and drove him off the plateau and also pushed the mixed detachment of both regiments away from the rearguard and off the hill. The best Tottenham could do was to rally at a wall half-way down the slope. Here he was reinforced by men collected by Napier and halted Molapo's advance. The Lancers had lost twenty men and were hard pressed. The Basuto swerved off to their right around the flank of the captured cattle and were charged by a troop of Lancers at the foot of the Berea, suffering casualties.'

Molapo had killed and wounded about fifteen per cent of Napier's force but had not managed to recapture the cattle.

He had, however, put Napier's men—who retired to the Caledon River camp—out of the fighting. Meanwhile Eyre had scaled the cliffs as ordered, but not without needless bloodshed. Before they started the climb his infantrymen had come upon a Basuto village and had killed several women and young girls: it is said in mitigation that the soldiers were used to fighting against the coast tribes on the eastern frontier who always evacuated non-combatants from the villages; whatever the excuse, the damage was done.

When Eyre reached the top he found himself, in his turn, among the cattle escaping from Napier's men. They managed to get together a herd of about fifteen hundred. While they were doing so a handful of Basuto wearing the white-covered undress caps and carrying lances of the 12th Lancers looted from the men who had been killed, infiltrated Eyre's troops. A Captain Faunce of the 73rd and three soldiers were unlucky enough to be taken prisoner. They were forced down the cliff path towards the Basuto village and there butchered by a hunch-back dwarf as a reprisal for the deaths of the women.

On the plateau Eyre had to face Molapo and the Basuto horse but by extending his men in a semi-circle and using his rockets he was able to hold on to the cattle. In the early afternoon heavy thunderstorms swept the Berea, causing the Basuto to seek shelter. About 4 p.m. Eyre was able to bring the cattle down and rendezvous with Cathcart on the plain. His losses had been slight.

Cathcart had marched south round the Berea without meeting any serious opposition and halted between the plateau and Thaba Bosiu. There he was joined by Eyre and, when the rain stopped, by about five thousand Basuto horsemen. They would not close but kept circling and wheeling as the howitzers dropped shell among them. Only a few casualties were inflicted. With evening drawing on Cathcart considered his position too exposed and he and Eyre fell back on a small village where they were able to pen the cattle in stone-walled kraals. Cathcart blamed Napier and Eyre for the setback. In despatches he complained of being left in the lurch while they had 'run wild after cattle', which he said did not accord with his orders. 'They are both fine fellows,' he wrote, 'but soldiers will easily see that the fault is not mine that we did not make a better job of it.'

As darkness deepened the Basutos closed in, shouting and singing to the cattle. There were some racing oxen among them trained to obey calls and these became restless.[1] About 8 p.m. they communicated their unease to the rest of the herd and four hundred frantic beasts burst out of the kraal and got away. All that night the troops stood to their arms but no further attacks were launched.

When morning came, there was not a Basuto in sight yet the threat of their presence was enough to force a decision on Cathcart. In his despatches he compared them to Circassians and Cossacks and the possibility that they might come riding down on him again caused him to move back to the camp on the Caledon River. The British had lost thirty-eight killed and fourteen wounded; the Basuto twenty dead and twenty wounded. It was during Cathcart's retreat that Moshesh produced one of the great diplomatic masterstrokes of African history. Not long after the British column had reached the river camp an envoy arrived with a letter which Moshesh, Casalis and Nehemiah had composed the previous night.

From the CHIEF MOSHESH to the HIGH COMMISSIONER.

Thaba Bosigo,
Midnight, 20 Dec. 1852.

Your Excellency,

This day you have fought against my people and taken much cattle. As the object for which you have come is to have a compensation for Boers, I beg you will be satisfied with what you have taken. I entreat peace from you—you have shown your power—you have chastised—let it be enough I pray you; and let me be no longer considered an enemy to the Queen. I will try all I can to keep my people in order in the future.

Your humble servant,
(Signed) MOSHESH

---

[1] This was a popular Basuto sport. The oxen would come to a call, a whistle, or to a particular chant and race riderless several miles to the home kraal. Pots of beer would be wagered on the outcome.

162

Why had Moshesh decided to turn victory into defeat, at least on paper? There is no doubt that the Basuto themselves were exhausted by the previous day's fighting and that he dreaded the renewal of hostilities. But above all he was a pragmatist, and Lagden, who lived in Lesotho for sixteen years, wrote: 'The fact was that both Generals (Cathcart and Moshesh) were sincerely anxious to find a way out of their dilemma and an excuse to call it "Peace". Moshesh had spent a miserable night. He was conscious of victory and dreaded its consequences more than defeat. Every time he saw one of his warriors decked in the garments of a Lancer it must have sent a pang through him, for he knew that the memory of the dead soldiers on the mountain, mutilated probably by his wild people against his wishes, would assuredly yield a harvest of vengeance from all white people, who abhorred the idea that blacks should prevail against whites. Yet, it was a fair enough fight to which no exception was or could be taken. Still, the Chief was stirred with the instinct that nothing but an heroic measure could save him from retribution at the hands of the British with whom at all times he wanted to be friendly, for he believed they meant well enough, though their methods were strange. In the dead of night he roused his missionary, M. Casalis, in whose presence he ordered his educated son, Nehemiah, to write down the inspired words of the letter. The inspiration was that he should accord to General Cathcart the honours of the day, admit chastisement and render homage.'

Cathcart quickly accepted Moshesh's offer. While the envoy waited he wrote a letter to the King in which he said, among other things, 'The words are those of a great chief. But I care little for words, I judge men by their actions. I told you if you did not pay the fine I must go and take it; I am a man who never breaks his word. I have taken the fine by force and I am satisfied . . . I now desire not to consider you, chief, as an enemy of the Queen, but I must proclaim martial law in the Sovereignty . . . for though you are a great chief, it seems that you either do not or can not keep your own people from stealing . . . now, therefore, Chief Moshesh, I consider your past obligation fulfilled.'

When Cathcart's reply and his attitude to Moshesh became

known in the camp there was considerable dissatisfaction. He was urged by his senior officers to return. For all his talk of war and the threat to take three times the number of cattle demanded as a fine, the force was now retiring with fewer cattle than had been demanded.

On December 22 Cathcart issued an Order of the Day in which he said, 'The Commander of the forces conveys his thanks to the Army engaged against the Basutos at the Berea on the 20th instant for their gallant conduct, and his admiration of their steadiness and discipline, by which an overwhelming host of Basutos and Bataungs were defeated, during a contest which lasted from early in the morning until 8 p.m. when the enemy, with a force of not less than six thousand well-armed horsemen, under considerable organization, after repeatedly assailing the troops at every point, was driven from the field with such severe loss as to compel him to sue for peace.' But no one was taken in. No matter how often Cathcart proclaimed victory, the men knew they had lost and were humiliated.

Moshesh, too, was in no doubt as to who had won and he made sure that the black peoples of South Africa learnt the truth. So rapid was communication between Moshesh and other tribal chiefs that King William's Town learnt the news of the Berea—the real news—two days before official despatches arrived.

In 1853 Moshesh turned on Sikonyela and his Batlokwa and drove them out of Lesotho. There were no reprisals. Moshesh was then sixty-seven. He was at the height of his power. He had defeated a British army and, with the possible exception of the Zulu king Mpande, he was the most powerful chief in South Africa. But he still had to face the Boers.

8

ALTHOUGH Cathcart had threatened martial law in the Sovereignty, it was an empty gesture. Just over a year after the Berea, a special commissioner, Sir George Clerk, signed the Bloemfontein Convention with the frontier farmers—much like the Sand River Convention—

this time stating that H.M. Government had no treaties with any chief other than Adam Kok and had no intention of making any that would hurt the farmers of the new 'Orange Free State'. With that the British marched away, pleased to be shaking the Free State dust from their boots. So the frontiers were now wide open—as they had been during the Sovereignty. The Free Staters set about the business of creating a State. A Volksraad (Parliament) was formed and in September, 1854, J. P. Hoffman was elected President. The cattle raiding on the Lesotho borders went on unchecked.

In Lesotho itself an event occurred which plunged the whole country into grief. Mrs Casalis—Ma-Eugene—died on June 17. Casalis described how chiefs and their councillors rode in from remote villages to pay their respects; many had been preceded by runners asking Casalis to delay burial as long as possible since they wished to see her once more. 'The bounds prescribed by my reverence for the dear remains were already past, while still others came to press kisses, bathed with tears, upon her forehead and all this passed in a land where the terrors inspired by death were such that one would have believed a house rendered forever uninhabitable, if in taking out a corpse it was not carried through a breach made at the end opposite the door!'

Two years later, in 1856, Casalis was recalled to take over the Mission House in Paris. By the time he wrote his moving account of life in Lesotho the Paris society had celebrated fifty years of field work there. During that time they had created schools, churches, an industrial college, a theological school, installed a printing press, built agricultural establishments, taught the Basuto how to cultivate wheat, potatoes and other vegetables; they had introduced the plough, had improved the strain of horses, sheep and bullocks and had seen Lesotho reach a point where it had a small export trade in cereals, wool and cattle.

In 1854, too, Cathcart left South Africa and was replaced by Sir George Grey. He had also been an army man but had resigned early and explored the coast of Western Australia before becoming governor of South Australia and later of New Zealand. He had earned a considerable reputation as an administrator, which was just as well, for one of the strangest and most pitiful chapters in South African history was about to be written; good administrators would be sorely needed.

In 1856 the Xhosa nation, one of the main Bantu tribes of South Africa, who lived on the eastern frontier of the Cape Colony several hundred miles to the south-east of Lesotho and who had been intermittently engaged in a series of exhausting wars—the Kaffir Wars—with British and Boer forces for more than thirty years, began to commit mass suicide. The tragedy has come to be known as the 'Cattle Killing' because much of the stock owned by the Xhosas was slaughtered on the advice of wizards. Its result was to have a profound effect on the economy of the Colony and was, overnight, to create a poverty-ridden slum where the Xhosas lived.

Moshesh has been held either wholly or in part responsible for the disaster. Short of any proof, one has to rely on theory and one such theory holds that Moshesh engineered the tragedy for two reasons. The first is that it was in line with his plan for a confederation of black against white and that it would unite the blacks once and for all. The second was that he now faced pressure from the Boers of the Orange Free State and as Professor Walker wrote, he 'proposed to keep the Colonists from helping the Republicans by giving them something to occupy themselves on their own borders'. If Moshesh was responsible, the deviousness of the scheme was in character for he was still keeping his options open as far as Britain was concerned. Had the confederation worked he would probably have been its leader, but he was realistic enough to recognize that it might not: in which case he wished to be allied to the strongest white group, the British.

In March, 1856, a seer called Mhlakaza and his daughter, Nonqause, began preaching to the Xhosas a doctrine of resurrection. Nonqause said she had spoken to the shades of old tribal heroes who pointed to the decay of their race through the oppression of the whites. They could no longer be silent spectators and it was their intention to rise again and save the Xhosas from extermination. However, there was a condition. They would only return if the entire Xhosa nation killed off all its cattle, leaving only horses and dogs. All grain was to be thrown away and no fields were to be cultivated. When these conditions had been fulfilled a great whirl-wind would blow across the land and sweep away all Xhosas who had refused to obey. Only then would the great warriors of the past rise up to take over the nation's destiny.

The news of the vision swept through southern Africa like a brush fire. Some whites refused to take it seriously. But one person was totally convinced that an enormous tragedy was brewing if nothing could be done to stop it. He was the Reverend Charles Brownlee, a missionary and administrator among the Gaikas, one of the tribes that made up the Xhosa nation. He worked tirelessly to damp down the spreading hysteria. He and his wife were later to write the only full accounts of the disaster.

Mrs Brownlee wrote, 'At first the kaffir nation was stunned. The sacrifice seemed too great. Tidings of the marvellous sights witnessed near Mhlakaza's village filled the country. The horns of oxen were said to be seen peeping from beneath the rushes which grew around a swampy pool near the village of the seer; and from a subterranean cave were heard the bellow-ing and knocking of the horns of cattle impatient to rise . . . There were those who said they had actually seen the risen heroes emerge from the Indian Ocean, some on foot, some on horseback, passing in silent parade before them, then sink-ing again among the tossings of the restless waves. Sometimes they were seen rushing through the air in the wild chase as of old. Then again they were seen marshalled in battle array. The horrors to befall the unbelievers were enlarged upon. White men would be turned into frogs, mice, and ants.

'One can imagine the effect of all this upon an intensely superstitious people.'

Brownlee used himself unsparingly. For months he spent almost every day in the saddle riding from village to village, reasoning, pleading and warning. Whenever they told him of the wonderful things that had been promised he always gave them a simple answer: 'Napakade' (never). He said it so many times that this became his name in Xhosa. In June 1856, he wrote to Colonel Maclean, his superior, saying among other things there was a rumour that 'Black Russians' had arrived. Rumours of the Crimean War had been current among the Xhosas from 1854 and they were convinced that the Russians were black people like themselves and that having fought the English in the Crimea they were coming south to fight them again and drive them into the sea. This rumour was given a certain credence when a rowing-boat was washed up on the coast containing a naval cap decorated with gold braid. The Xhosas assured themselves that the Russians had killed the British crew.

Brownlee was worried that violent incidents involving white people might occur and wrote that travellers should take the utmost precaution. 'I do not think any solitary or unprotected traveller is safe and it would be well for traders and others who cross the Kei, to travel under the protection of some influential Kaffir.' But for all his efforts the killing of cattle and the destruction of stored grain began.

Mrs Brownlee wrote of the delusion: 'Wonderful reports were constantly in circulation. Armies were seen reviewing on the sea, others sailing in umbrellas; thousands of cattle were heard knocking their horns together and bellowing in caverns, impatient to rise, only waiting until all their fellows who still walked the earth were slain; dead men years in the grave had been seen, who sent pathetic appeals to their kindred not to delay their coming back to life by refusing to obey the prophet. Cattle were then killed, feasting was the order of the day, but it was impossible to consume all. Dogs were gorged on fat beef, vultures were surfeited, whole carcasses were left to putrefy, the air became tainted with corruption. Alas! Later on it was the carcasses of men and women, young men and maidens, children and infants that strewed the wayside. Oh, the sadness of it all.'

The Brownlees bought one thousand bags of maize to store at the then price of about five shillings a bag. As famine gripped the area the price rose to two pounds and three pounds a bag and even at those prices it was often impossible to find it.

Brownlee had been desperately working on the Gaika chief Sandile and early on managed to restrain him from ordering his people to destroy their food stocks, in spite of pressure on him by his mother, who is reported as sending him a message stating, 'It is all very well for you, Sandile. You have your wives and children, but I am solitary. I am longing to see my husband; you are keeping him from rising by your disobedience to the command of the spirits.'

In January, 1857, ten months after the beginning of the delusion, Nonqause ordered that all cattle be killed within eight days. 'It was a week of painful anxiety,' wrote Mrs Brownlee. 'I feared for my husband's life, as many of the evildisposed were very bitter against him, and they believed it was his influence that kept Sandile from obeying the prophet.'

In expectation of the start of a millennium the Xhosas cleaned out their empty cattle kraals and corn pits, enlarging them and making them stronger to hold the coming bounty. Many huts were re-thatched and strengthened to resist the expected whirlwind.

'The eighth day came on which the heaven and earth were to come together amid darkness, thunder, lightning, rain, and a mighty wind, by which the Amagogotya (unbelievers) together with the white man would be driven into the sea,' wrote Mrs Brownlee. 'At the dawn of the great day a nation, many of whom had doubtless not slept, rose joyfully, decked themselves with paint, beads and rings, to welcome their long-lost friends. One of the saddest sights was that of an old woman wizened with age, and doubly wrinkled by starvation, decked out with brass rings jingling on her withered arms and legs. They had kept on their ornaments hoping against hope, till too weak to remove them. The sun rose and made the circuit of the heavens closely watched by expectant hosts in vain. He set in silent majesty in the west, leaving the usual darkness over the earth, and the black darkness of a bitter disappointment in the hearts of thousands.' Within days people began to die. Food, anything edible at all, was at a premium.

Not every Xhosa had destroyed his cattle and grain. All of one Sunday the Brownlees watched herds being driven past their house by Xhosas wishing to put as many miles and a military post or two between themselves and the starving thousands.

Those who had destroyed their property soon weakened and sat all day in their villages. Each morning they would walk or crawl to the cattle kraals and corn pits hoping to see them full. Each morning they were disappointed. Bones which they had

169

thrown away in days of plenty were now gathered and gnawed. Women and children wandered across the veld digging for roots—so assiduously that the whole area became pot-holed and unsafe for riding. Messengers were sent to the worst-affected areas telling the people they could get food either on farms owned by whites or in the nearest towns, but many still hung on and it was not until hundreds had died that the movement towards the Colony began. 'Those who reached us were most pitiable figures,' wrote Mrs Brownlee. 'Breathing skeletons, with hollow eyes and parched lips. The innocent children looked like old men and women in miniature, some only a few days old.' The land was covered with dead and dying. It was summer and the possibility of disease was real. The Government gave half a crown to anyone who found a body and buried it. Soup kitchens were set up, corn and meat were distributed, but for many the help had come too late.

It is not easy to give exact figures, but the most likely estimates are that between a hundred and fifty and two hundred thousand cattle were killed. This led to a death rate from famine and disease of between twenty and thirty thousand people. The population of certain chiefdoms between the Kei and Fish Rivers was estimated to have dropped from 104,721 in January, 1857, to 37,697 in December—a loss of over sixty-seven thousand. Of this total about thirty thousand moved into the Colony for employment. Some went as migrant labourers and later returned. Others settled on farms in the eastern Cape and their descendants have remained there as farm servants ever since.

In recent years another theory has been advanced for the catastrophe—that the Xhosas acted as they did in expectation of the millennium. In his book, *The Trumpet Shall Sound*, a study of millenarism, and in particular the 'Cargo Cults' of Melanesia, Peter Worsley wrote: 'The basic condition (for the emergence of a millenarian movement) is a situation of dissatisfaction with existing social conditions and yearnings for a happier life ... It is no accident that the millenarian idea, when introduced into suitable situations in societies where the idea itself was previously absent, has flourished like the bay tree.' And again: 'There is (another) type of social situation in which activist millenarian ideas are likely to flourish. This is when a society with differentiated political institutions is fighting for its existence by quite secular military–political means, but is meeting with defeat after defeat. One may cite the case of the rise of the prophet Nonqause at a time when the Xhosa people were beginning to realize that they were losing the long-drawn-out Kaffir Wars.'

The most obvious parallels are the two great waves of Ghost Dance among the American Indians in 1870 and 1890, when prophets promised the return of the dead if people would abandon sin and adopt the cult. The Sioux, who had suffered severely from the loss of tribal lands and the disappearance of the buffalo, emberked on this with such fervour that the massacre at Wounded Knee resulted, in which 300 out of 370 Sioux were butchered by machine-gun fire. There are also parallels among the 'Cargo-Cults' where property is destroyed in expectation of the return of dead heroes. And there is a ringing echo of Dona Beatriz in the Old Kingdom, whose way to a Golden Age also lay in invoking the past. She, however, foresaw the future in terms of a new religion, not as an age built on a framework of self-destruction. The parallels go further; the Old Kingdom was in a state of disorder and decay brought on largely by white pressure. The Xhosas, who had fought a series of losing wars over a long period, had seen their tribal lands diminish, and had become more and more densely packed as their area of land grew less.

Millenarism may have been partly responsible for the 'Cattle Killing', but several major historians nominate Moshesh as the villain. Cory states flatly: 'War, due to the Basutos stealing Free State cattle and the farmers' retaliations, was always impending . . . And it was noticed that when war . . . became more imminent, activity in the cattle killing became more intense. When in August (1858) the Free State Boers made an expedition against a robber chief Witzie, in which Moshesh was in no way involved . . . there was such a lull in cattle killing that it appeared . . . (it) had quite died down . . . But when Moshesh expected attacks prophecies were most abundant. Moshesh therefore must have been acting either directly or indirectly with Mhlakaza . . .'

9

MOSHESH was growing old; at the time of the Cattle Killing he was seventy, and was vulnerable to his family now that Casalis had gone. He had had a series of wives over the years, and some of his own children were younger than some of his grandchildren. His sons were proud. They had seen a British army advance on their country and go away defeated; they had seen their tribe's fame act as a magnet to other tribes; alliances had been made, knees bent, vassalage acknowledged. The Affair at the Berea had given the Basuto a new stature: Moshesh's sons became conscious of their power and arrogantly raided into the Free State. There were constant forays in search of easy pickings and the infant Boer state grew more and more apprehensive. As Tylden said, 'There was no real safety for either life or property (in the Free State) and the extent of a man's holding was usually little more than the range of his gun or rifle.' From this period dates a story which has been retold, changing only its locale, in every African emergency since. A farmer's wife asked her Basuto servants if, in the event of war, they would kill her and her children. She was told that their job would be to kill the neighbouring family, whose servants would perform the same office for their employers. Jan Fick, one of the best-known and toughest men in the Winburg district was quoted as saying, 'I have been fighting kaffirs since I was eleven years old, when my father's house was burnt down in a kaffir outbreak and we had to fight for our lives in the veld.' The result was that in 1857 when a permanent executive was set up in the Orange Free State and a constitution adopted, one of the provisions was that there would be no equality in Church or State between black and white.

Like Lesotho, the Free State had its renegades and adventurers, and the executive was unable to do much to restrain them. There were no real prisons and it was difficult to bring offenders to justice. The position of the Landdrosts (magistrates) was so precarious that they feared to hand down corrective sentences on whites who might have influence behind them. The Landdrost of Winburg was savagely attacked by a white farmer when he gave judgement against him. The farmer felled him with a blow from the butt of his horse-pistol then tried to strangle him.

In an attempt to keep the peace, President Hoffman, who was living on a farm given him by Moshesh, had sent as his first ambassador to the Court of Thaba Bosiu, Joseph Millard Orpen, a man of integrity who was farming in the Free State. Orpen, an Irishman born in Dublin in 1828, eventually became one of the Basuto's most ardent champions, married twice—both times into French missionary families—and died aged ninety-seven in 1925. He succeeded in maintaining the *status quo* for a year or two but things were gradually accelerating towards a confrontation.

One of the most arrogant of Basuto cattle raiders was Moshesh's brother, Poshuli. In February, 1858, on the pretence of hunting, he and a large party made a showy display in a disputed area and ejected a Boer family from their farm. This had immediate repercussions: the Free State seethed with rumours, alarmist reports were sent to Bloemfontein, and the farmers took their families into laagers—the traditional fortified wagon camps which the Voortrekkers had used so successfully in times of attack. Attempts were made on both sides to take the heat out of the situation but they were unavailing. The weeks dragged by. The laagers became dirty and insanitary. There was fear of disease. A state of war existed without the war itself.

Lagden wrote: 'The two races were on the brink of war. It was not that they hated each other so much as that they were the victims of much misunderstanding, partly due to the vagaries of British policy, partly to the scheming of land-grabbers and adventurers who too often got the approval of Major Warden and other officials for occupying ground which the natives were forbidden to expropriate and the Government had no power to give away. A succession of governors made treaties, laws, boundaries and pledges which were alternately confirmed and disallowed. Inspired by the best intentions they created problems and pirouetted around them.'

173

On March 11, 1858, the first Boer–Basuto war broke out, called the Month's War. The President of the Free State, then Boshoff, made a formal declaration claiming the Warden Line. About a thousand men were put into the field armed with percussion-cap smooth-bore guns and seven small pieces of ordnance of which little use was made. The force split into two columns, one under Commandant Senekal entering Lesotho from the north, the other under Commandant Weber from the south. Senekal tried to cross the Caledon River where the British had crossed four years previously, at Cathcart's Drift, but his force was faced by six thousand Basuto who attacked unrelentingly for forty-eight hours, killing seventeen Boers and hurling them back across the river. They finally moved downstream to link up with the southern column.

Weber had had an equally disastrous start, disastrous in the sense that what he had done would from then on be stigmatized a Boer atrocity: he had attacked the French Protestant Mission of Beersheba on the farm Zevenfontein which had been established twenty years before on land given by Moshesh himself. The attack came as a shock to French and Basuto alike for the Boers were known to be a devoutly Christian people, puritan and Calvinistic. But they disliked missionaries. They considered that the London Missionary Society in particular, and missionaries in general, tended to take the side of black against white and that those blacks who had lengthy contact with missionary stations became insolent, lazy and so made unattractive labourers. Naturally there are two accounts of what happened. According to the Boer version the station was considered a menace to Weber's lines of communication and a force under a man called Sauer, who was the Smithfield magistrate, surrounded it at daylight and called on the residents four times in the space of two hours to surrender their arms. The Basuto inmates refused, became hostile; the Boers opened fire, killing thirty and capturing three thousand head of cattle. In the version of M. Rolland, head of the mission, one summons was given to surrender with a time limit of only five minutes. He stated he was still trying to get together the arms to hand over when the building was hit by a hail of bullets. Ten people who fled from the mission and stumbled

174

into a ravine for shelter were hunted down and shot. The station was then pillaged. Whichever version was preferred, what is important is the fact that a French Protestant mission was attacked at all. The French missionaries had achieved a unique relationship with the Basuto and had the sympathetic ear of both the French and British Governments; it was something the Boers never seemed to realize, something that eventually would work against them.

Moshesh did not move. He sat on the top of his mountain and let the two forces come towards him, drawing them farther and farther from the Free State. Then, at a place called The Hell because of its brooding ugliness, an element of Weber's force foolishly went after a decoy herd of cattle. Moshesh's son Letsie cut them off, surrounded them and attacked them with the terrifying Basuto throwing axe. Although the Basuto lost more than sixty men in the skirmish and the Boers only fifteen the *pro rata* loss to the Boers was the more serious for they had no reserves to draw on. On 25 April, 1858 the north and south columns met and moved towards Thaba Bosiu under Senekal's overall command. When they reached Casalis's first mission station at Moriah, a terrible sight confronted them; they found the mutilated corpses of their comrades who had been killed at The Hell. The bodies had been badly hacked about and portions were missing. It was Basuto custom to remove parts of their dead enemies to make a strengthening medicine for their own men. Under the circumstances it is not surprising that the mission was sacked. Again there are two versions: the Boers said that Arbousset, Casalis's original companion, and several English traders had helped the Basuto and encouraged them. Arbousset, on the other hand, claimed that he and the traders had taken refuge in a cave and had had no part in the fighting.[1]

The Boer force, numbering only about nine hundred men because of desertions, moved on Thaba Bosiu. They found

[1] Appealed to by the French mission, the British Government refused compensation on the ground that the war had nothing to do with Britain, but the Free State Government eventually paid £100 towards the construction of a new school building.

every pass blocked and defended. Moshesh now counter-attacked by sending raiding parties into the Free State where they wrecked farmsteads and drove off cattle. It was what the Boers had feared most. More began to desert. There was a proposal to storm Thaba Bosiu. It was refused. Men drifted away, fearful of what was happening to their families. The force became weaker and weaker. On June 1 the Free State president had no option but to ask Moshesh for an armistice.

Once again, as with the outcome of the British attack, the resultant propaganda was wide of the truth. Rumours of victory swept across the Free State; some claimed that the Boers had achieved what they had set out to achieve: they had captured great herds of cattle and chastised the Basuto. Moshesh wrote a letter to the Free State president when the Boer desertions were at their height that is a classic of African satire. It began:

> Good Friend,
> I, Moshesh, do greet you, Boshoff, my chief and master. Your messenger came in last night with a letter, in which your Honour begins to speak of peace. I am sorry that you ever spoke of war. It is not Moshesh who began the war, and I must add that I have not fought any battle as yet.

It is a very long letter and must have made excessively irritating reading for the Free State president. Moshesh was quite agreeable to overtures of peace, but he was not going to be done out of his lecture. He took Boshoff to task on the grounds of cowardice as well as the professed Christianity of the Boers, both bitter pills to swallow. Another section reads:

> Oh, my good chief Boshoff, call in the captains of your late commando, and rebuke them much, for they have done you much harm in their march through my country.
> You style yourself a Christian in your last letter to me. I knew long since that you were a Christian, but the captains of your warriors are not, for if you persisted in saying that they also are Christians, we would immediately conclude that there is no God. What! Does their Christianity consist in destroying Christianity?

Another section reads:

176

As the winter is drawing near, I wish that your deputation would soon come, because in case we could not agree, we must go on with the war, for the sooner we fight the better for all parties, in order that after the great battle is over we may retire into some winter quarters ... The reports of your commandos and correspondents which are published in *The Friend* (a Bloemfontein newspaper which still exists) are wonderful inventions, and therefore they are utterly false.

However, some burghers of the Free State might take them to be faithful and trustworthy statements, and taking for granted that we have been greatly and easily defeated, they might in succeeding years be inclined to incite wars against us, perhaps for very specious reasons. Moreover, these statements have hurt the feelings of our warriors, whom I had great trouble to keep within bounds during the present struggle.

The English know that we are no cowards and we would like the Boers to learn that we know how to fight for our rights ... and then perhaps peace would be a little more sincere on the part of the Boers.

In his reply, Boshoff made no reference to the true state of affairs, but there is an illuminating letter from him to the resident magistrate of Aliwal North in which he said: 'The Boers, by their unaccountable sudden break-up, have brought me in such a fix as I never yet was in all my life. They imagine that they have given Moshesh such a licking that he will keep quiet for many a day, poor fools.'

10

ANOTHER GOVERNOR; another boundary conference; 1864. This time the new British Governor was Sir Philip Wodehouse, and there was a new president of the Orange Free State, an extremely able man, Jan Hendrik Brand. And, of course, Moshesh. As in Greek drama, the myth remains constant, the end never varies, only the actors change. A new border was defined, more paper was signed, more promises were made—and broken. The difference this time was that the Basuto considered themselves hard done by and another war became inevitable. However, before it broke out, Moshesh passed a law which was one of the cornerstones on which Lesotho was built and to which the country in great measure owes its present existence. It is known as 'The Law for Trade' and once and for all sums up the attitude of a black African king towards the land of which the kingdom was composed: 'I, Moshesh, write for any trader, whoever he may be, already in my land, and for any who may come to trade with the Basutos; my word is this: Trade to me and my tribe is a good thing. I wish to promote it. Any trader who wishes to establish a shop must first obtain permission from me. Should he build a house, I grant him no right to sell it. Further, I do not grant him liberty to plough the fields but only to plant a small vegetable garden. The trader who fancies that the place he is sojourning in belongs to him must dismiss the thought, if not, he is to quit; for there is no place belonging to the whites in my land; and I have granted no white man a place, either by word, or by writing.' When Britain eventually took over Lesotho as a protectorate she based her informal policy on this philosophy.

But at the time the immediate future of Lesotho was dominated by the desires of her white neighbour. Brand was elected president of the Free State in 1864 and inherited a country torn by dissension and restlessness. It has been said that he foresaw a new war against the Basuto as the only way of uniting his people; if that is so, his ideas on statecraft seem to run parallel with those of Moshesh. He also foresaw the difficulty of bringing a country to economic maturity without a port; his munitions, for instance, had to come up all the way from Port Elizabeth, a British-controlled port, by ox wagon. If he could launch a sudden attack on fortress-Lesotho, take its rich lands, he might then be able to roll down towards the coast, opening up a Boer corridor to Port St Johns. It was an imperial dream. On May 29, 1865, he tried to turn it into reality.

To the Basuto the second war with the Free State is known as the 'War of the Noise of Cannon'. To the Free State, 'The Great War'. This time the white republic was better prepared:

her army varied between two thousand five hundred and four thousand men with mercenary detachments of Hottentots and Bantu hostile to the Basuto. The Boers had replaced their muskets with rifles and were magnificent shots; they also had a number of field guns but were as yet unsophisticated in their use. The Basuto on the other hand were less militarily efficient than they had been eight years before. Their most obvious disadvantage was Moshesh's age: he was nearly eighty and was slipping away. The Black Confederation had come to nothing and he had transformed his allegiance totally to Britain. His great desire—one he had had all his adult life—was still to be taken under her wing and it had now become an obsession. However, Britain had no plans to add Lesotho to the Empire. Only a few years before, Moshesh had maintained to Orpen that Queen Victoria would not desert her children, thereby putting himself in a totally false position, for while she had black 'children' in many parts of the world, Moshesh was still unadopted. He always said he wanted to be her soldier, and to have her represented at Thaba Bosiu. His sons did not share his feelings and because they no longer felt his grip they did more or less what they pleased. The land was not united under a single hand any longer. Still, it was a formidable nation; it could put between ten and twenty thousand mounted warriors into the field and though they were less well-armed than the Boers, they outnumbered them at least five to one. And they had made reasonable preparations; a number of fortified mountains were stocked with grain, and cattle had been hidden in the high valleys.

Once again the attack was made by two columns, one led by Jan Fick, the second by Louw Wepener and after one or two minor skirmishes they joined up before Thaba Bosiu having 'annexed' portions of Lesotho on the way. It was one of the consistent weaknesses of Boer armies that the men were highly individualistic, untrained in the acceptance of orders, and prone to group loyalties. This time there were many in Wepener's column who resented the overall command going to Fick, and things were made worse by the fact that the two commanders did not like each other. Once again the magic of Thaba Bosiu began to work. As they laagered below it, a superstitious depression swept the Boer rank and file. The

Mountain of Night had never been taken: would it again prove too much for them? On August 8 Fick ordered Wepener to attack the Raebe Pass on the southern face. After the Boer cannon had silenced Moshesh's artillery Wepener and a thousand men assaulted the mountain. But half way up he committed a fatal error; he changed his plan of attack. The men faltered, some retired. Others stayed where they were. Only eight men reached the top and they had to scramble down to safety when they discovered that no one was willing to support them. Six days later, Wepener led another attack, but morale had suffered in the interim. Of the six hundred men who were to follow him, only three hundred actually did so and some of these stayed behind at the foot of the hill.

This time there was no rush to the top but a steady advance from rock to rock, bush to bush, firing, reloading, firing, reloading. The fissure up which the Boers were advancing became narrower as it neared the summit, which meant that the men had to bunch together. Stones and boulders began to crash down on them and by afternoon only about one hundred men were left unwounded. But they were doing well. The fissure had been blocked by three stone walls, two of which had been taken. The third was held by one of Moshesh's sons and some of the best warriors. At 5 p.m. Wepener climbed out on to a flat rock near this wall to open his field of fire, and was shot dead by a volley from the Basuto. Wessels, the second-in-command, then tried to force the wall and he, too, was shot. The Basuto counter-attacked and the disheartened Boers surged down the fissure in a panicky horde. Wessels, badly wounded, managed to get clear with difficulty. Of the three hundred stormers who had started with Wepener, eleven had been killed and nine seriously wounded. The Basuto losses were light.

Although, in the years to come, the Free State developed new tactics and acquired more powerful weapons, they never again tried to capture Thaba Bosiu. It was one of the mountain's ironies that its reputation outstripped reality. Had the Boers known what panic their attacks caused they might have renewed them with success. Letters from French missionaries described the conditions on the mountain during the following days as deplorable. Moshesh had collected a vast herd of cattle on the top, thinking his people would forget their divisions and fight for the common wealth of the nation. Thaba Bosiu was soon in a fearful state. The springs were unable to cope with the demand and the cattle, maddened by hunger and thirst, died in thousands, their dead bodies being used as barricades. With the summit one stinking mass of decaying flesh—four thousand carcasses were counted later —and the probability of disease, Moshesh wrote to the Free State president suggesting that Sir Philip Wodehouse be called in as mediator. The president seemed to think that the Free State had won the battle, for the terms he demanded were extraordinarily harsh. Forty thousand head of cattle, five thousand horses, and sixty thousand sheep, to be delivered in four days; the land which Wepener and Fick had 'annexed' to go to the Free State; a Boer magistrate to sit at Thaba Bosiu; all arms and ammunition to be given up; and two of Moshesh's sons to be sent as hostages until the peace treaty was signed.

It was impossible for Moshesh to comply. In a letter to Wodehouse in which he criticized what he called unreasonable conditions there was the following paragraph: 'Another condition imposed upon me is that I must become subject to the Free State; but I will never do so. I consider myself subject to the British Government and I hope Your Excellency shall take interest in my cause, and come to establish peace as soon as possible, as I am determined the Government of the Free State will never have my country. I am, therefore, giving myself and my country up to Her Majesty's Government under certain conditions which we may agree upon between Your Excellency and me.'

While Moshesh awaited a reply from Cape Town—it was unfavourable, for the British Government did not wish to increase its holdings in South Africa at the time—the Transvaal entered the war on the side of the Free State and the laagers at the foot of Thaba Bosiu were disbanded. But this time the Boers did not go home. Instead they split up into commandos and began a series of *chevauchees*, quartering the country, rounding up its cattle, fighting wherever an enemy force showed. In April, 1866, a kind of peace was signed but only so that both sides could get the harvest in, and by

February, 1867, Moshesh and his sons felt themselves strong enough to renew the struggle to regain land they had lost. By July, Free State commandos were again in the field and what was known as the 'Little War' began. These commandos harried the Basuto much as the Koranas had done; they burnt crops, drove off cattle, made lightning raids on villages. The Basuto became refugees in their own country. Those who could, travelled to the mountain fortresses for safety. Hunger, the old enemy, returned and with it cannibalism. Moshesh for once had no answer. Though there was food in various parts of Lesotho there was no means of distributing it. People began to die of starvation. Moshesh, in despair, began bombarding Wodehouse with requests for help.

Wodehouse was sympathetic. For some time he had been in favour of Lesotho's annexation by Britain and, indeed, had requested it. So, too, was the British Civil Commissioner at Aliwal North, Mr John Burnet. Two years previously, at the end of the 'Great War', he had visited Thaba Bosiu and had written to Wodehouse, 'Moshesh is done mentally. All is disorganization and jealousy among the greater Chiefs, who as well as the petties find the reins slipping from their hands. The great mass of the people are tired, worn out by the oppression and bad government of the Chiefs; and I am persuaded that the whole of Basutoland is ripe, rotten ripe, for falling into the hands of the Queen's Government if a plan could be found.'

In one last desperate appeal to Wodehouse for annexation by Britain, Moshesh described himself and his nation as being 'the lice in the Queen's blanket'. Again Wodehouse pressed the British Government and in January, 1868, received a document from the Duke of Buckingham and Chandos, Secretary of State for the Colonies, authorizing the annexation of Lesotho to the British colony of Natal—not the Cape, as Wodehouse had hoped. But it was enough. Wodehouse told the Free State president that hostilities would now cease. The annexation was only just in time. The Boers had done what they had never managed before: by their guerrilla tactics, they had almost conquered Lesotho. The rugged land had been reduced by perpetual harassment but the symbol of its identity, Thaba Bosiu, still stood like some Krak de Chevalier, when all around the people had been defeated. On March 12, what Moshesh had so fervently wished occurred. Wodehouse issued the following proclamation:

Whereas with a view to the restoration of peace and future maintenance of tranquillity and good government on the north-eastern Border of the Colony of the Cape of Good Hope, Her Majesty the Queen has been graciously pleased to comply with the request made by Moshesh, the Paramount Chief, and other Headmen of the tribe of the Basutos, that the said tribe may be admitted into the Allegiance of Her Majesty; and whereas Her Majesty has been further pleased to authorize me to take the necessary steps for giving effect to Her pleasure in the Matter:

Now, therefore, I do hereby proclaim and declare that from and after the publication hereof the said tribe of the Basutos shall be, and shall be taken to be, for all intents and purposes, British subjects; and the territory of the said tribe shall be, and shall be taken to be, British Territory. And I hereby require all Her Majesty's subjects in South Africa to take notice of this my Proclamation accordingly.

God Save the Queen!

Although in the years ahead Lesotho was also to be ruled by the Cape Colony before coming under direct British rule this was the beginning of the country's long journey to its present unique position, that of an independent, multi-racial black kingdom poised in the very heart of a country whose policies are diametrically opposed.

But Lesotho had paid a heavy price; thousands of Basuto had been killed in the fighting, some had died of starvation, tens of thousands of cattle had been lost. In one sense a certain justice had been meted out for their years of border raiding. Their morale as a nation was temporarily shattered. On April 15 Wodehouse held a *Pitso*, a national assembly of the Basuto nation, about twenty miles from Maseru, where Moshesh made his unequivocal surrender to Queen Victoria. 'The country is dead', the old man said. 'We are all dead, take us and do what you like with us.'

183

In the Free State, the farmers were bitter. A whole new country had lain open before them; now it was closed for ever.

It was as though Moshesh had willed himself to live until the future of his country was secure, for once Wodehouse made his proclamation Moshesh's strength began to fail and he declined rapidly. He found it difficult to remain awake and would often fall into a doze even when guests were present. Once when Wodehouse visited him, the King told him he expected to die soon and was glad to know his people were safe. Wodehouse was greatly affected by the old man's frailty. Moshesh asked him to describe the new boundaries of the kingdom but fell asleep as he was doing so.

The months passed. Moshesh spent much of his time dozing beneath a pile of skins. When important visitors arrived at Thaba Bosiu he made an effort to gather what strength he had left; with their departure he would slip more deeply into lassitude and senility. As he approached his death, he became obsessed by a need to embrace the Christian faith. He decided to be baptized by the missionaries and March 12, 1870, was chosen. A huge platform was built at his insistence so that everyone might witness the event. For days beforehand, thousands of Basutos made their way along the mountain tracks. Two days before the baptism was due, Thaba Bosiu was thronged by people. But Moshesh died in his sleep on March 11, simply slipping away in the early dawn in the presence of two of his sons. Those who had come to rejoice with him stayed to mourn his passing. He is buried on Thaba Bosiu. Tylden wrote a fitting epitaph: 'Since his death he has become to the Basuto the incarnation of all their most cherished traditions and most of their characteristics, as well as the originator of their prosperity.'

* * *

The story of Lesotho does not end with the death of Moshesh, nor was its future a path strewn with roses.[1] But it is the

[1] The Cape Government took over Lesotho in 1871 and in 1880 tried to disarm the people. The Basutos rose in rebellion and what has come to be called 'The Gun War' ensued, which lasted for about a year. In 1884 the country was transferred directly to the Crown and came under the authority of the Colonial Office.

watershed. There was a saying among the Boers during the 'Little War' that it was 'a rifle and a bush and a range of six hundred yards that beat the Basuto'. Looking back now, one does not see things in those simplistic terms. While Moshesh lived on his mountain, the Basuto were never beaten. By the time he died he had, in effect, passed the paramountcy of his people to the fierce old Queen across the water—whom no one beat. Moshesh and Casalis had stood together for a long time, but finally it was only Moshesh who was left to withstand the pressure. Unlike the Old Kingdom of Congo, which opened its arms to the white man too widely, unlike the Kingdom of Dahomey, which shut its doors too firmly, Moshesh was a man who understood whites; they were, in the long run, no different from himself. But he also had luck; there was Casalis and there was the length of his own life. It seems unlikely that, had he died at three score years and ten, his sons could have saved their country. And so, one might say that it was a mountain and a man who beat the Boers.

11

MOSHESH'S GREAT-GRANDSON, Moshoeshoe II, is the present King of Lesotho. He is in his thirties, a slender, good-looking man with his forebear's aquiline features. He was educated in Britain and now lives in the former British residency. He has a passion, like many Basutos, for racehorses.

When Lesotho became independent in 1966 King Moshoeshoe left Oxford in the midst of his studies and returned home to lead his people. But things had changed since his great-grandfather's day. Politicians had taken over the old functions of village headman and court adviser, and he found himself isolated from the people he wished to lead. He persisted in his endeavour, provoked a trial of strength between himself and the politicians and soon found himself in exile in Holland. There he finally acknowledged that the role of kingship had changed and was allowed to return to Lesotho as a constitutional monarch.

The country itself is ruled by the Basotho National Party,

but in effect by the King's uncle, Chief Leabua Jonathan who, as Prime Minister, seems at the time of writing (1974) to be redesigning the structure of Lesotho politics into a one-party state.

The future of the country is uncertain. One view holds that it is a land of vanishing freedoms, that law and order will eventually break down and that it will become a black slum more and more dependent upon South Africa, where ninety per cent of its able-bodied men presently find employment. A more optimistic assessment suggests that it is on the point of a great leap forward. Seven new luxury hotels are planned to cope with an expected tourist boom. De Beers, the diamond giant, has bought a twenty-five per cent holding in a new diamond mine in the north. A huge dam is planned to enable Lesotho to sell water to the thirsty industrial areas of South Africa.

Neither view is much in evidence to the casual traveller in Lesotho today. I first visited the country more than twenty years ago, when it was ruled by young men of the Colonial Service. The capital, Maseru, which lies about fifteen miles from Thaba Bosiu on the Caledon River, was a hamlet with dusty, rutted streets; what buildings existed were constructed of dressed mountain stone and red corrugated-iron roofs. It had not changed much since the Earl of Rosslyn stayed with Sir Godfrey Lagden—commissioner for sixteen years—during the Boer War. In his book, *Twice Captured,* the Earl described the Residency as 'a nice comfortable little bungalow', and said, 'the Government offices are also worth looking at, but I cannot claim any desire to live there for sixteen years . . .'

In those days there were less than a hundred whites in Maseru, today there are several thousand in Lesotho, many of them traders, but also a significant group of diplomats and representatives of United Nations organizations. Maseru still has an impermanent frontier look. Its main street—there are few others—is lined with a mixture of old and new buildings, none more than two or three storeys, and it is easy to pick out the solid structures of the colonial period. Basuto horse-men wrapped against the mountain cold in coloured blankets, still ride their ponies into town and tether them along the main street in grassy vacant lots which, according to the roadside signs, are eventually to be developed as the headquarters of this or that ministry.

Down a side road is a brash American hotel, part of a worldwide chain, that is the centre of Maseru's social life. It stands above the Caledon River, a glass and concrete structure, new, raw, but already exerting an influence that has spread beyond the borders of Lesotho. Here one can buy porno best-sellers and girlie magazines, banned in South Africa, see the latest movies uncut by a South African censor, play roulette and blackjack and, in the darkened American bars, pick up black girls. Across the river in South Africa such practices are not only illegal but, if pursued, would carry gaol sentences.

It is instructive to watch *apartheid* break down under these pressures. Each weekend the hotel is filled with Moshesh's old enemies, Free State farmers. The magazines and books disappear from the racks, the casino is packed with whites jostling the local blacks for a place at the tables, assignations are quickly made. (When I was there a new rule was made banning single women from both the casino and the bars.)

While Maseru must act as a kind of pressure valve to frustrated South Africans, the sight of whites throwing their money about, dominating the fruit-machines and the gaming tables, racing down the newly tarred roads in their big American and German cars, has produced the opposite effect among the Basuto. The country is one of the ten poorest on earth and it is not surprising that the wealth of its surrounding neighbour has activated feelings of envy and dislike even above the natural dislike of its *apartheid* philosophy.

One is aware of a sense of uneasiness among whites either living or touring in Lesotho. Many traders employ night-watchmen to guard their homes from burglars; shop assistants, hotel receptionists, government civil servants all made one feel barely tolerated. Herd boys on lonely country roads offer black power salutes to whites driving by.

But these are pinpricks that will resolve themselves in time, and time is on the side of the Basuto. The royal house, if subdued, is healthy; the state exists and, with luck, will become more viable, and it is in South Africa's interest to help where it can.

The abiding impressions one carries away are of the beauty

187

of the country itself: smoke rising from a hillside village as the evening cooking fires are lit; golden yellow cliffs glowing in the early sunshine; blue-black thunderstorms sweeping across the Berea plateau at noon; and, as one crosses the narrow bridge that takes one into South Africa and sees the first 'Whites Only' notice on the customs post, the impressions give place to a simple feeling of wonder—that Lesotho has survived at all.

SOME SOURCE BOOKS

The Kingdom of Congo

Armattoe, Dr R. E. G. *The Golden Age of West African Civilization* (Lomeshie Research Centre, 1946)

Axelson, Eric *Congo to Cape. Early Portuguese Explorers* (London 1973)

Balandier, Georges *Daily Life in the Kingdom of the Kongo* (Trans. Helen Weaver, London 1968)

Boxer, C. R. *The Old Kingdom of Congo*, in *The Dawn of African History*, edited by Roland Oliver (London 1961)

Bush, M. L. *Renaissance, Reformation and the Outer World* (London 1967)

Childs, G. M. *Umbundu Kinship and Character* (London 1949)

Davidson, Basil *The African Awakening* (London 1955) *Black Mother* (London 1961)

Duffy, James *Portuguese Africa* (London 1949)

Egerton, F. C. *Angola in Perspective* (London 1957)

Eppstein, John *Does God Say Kill?* (London 1972)

Lopez, Duarte *see* Pigafetta

Parry, J. H. *The European Reconnaissance* (New York 1968)

Pigafetta, F. and Lopez, D. *A Report of the Kingdom of Congo* (trans. and ed. by M. Hutchinson, London 1881)

Ravenstein, E. G. *The Strange Adventures of Andrew Battell* (Hakluyt Soc.)
The Voyages of Cão and Bartholomew Dias 1482–88 (Geographical Journal, London 1900)

Wheeler, D. L. and Pelissier, R. *Angola* (London 1971)

The Kingdom of Dahomey

Akinjogbin, I. A. *Dahomey and its Neighbours 1708–1818* (London 1967)

Argyle, W. J. *The Fon of Dahomey* (London 1966)

Burton, Sir R. *A Mission to Gelele, King of Dahome* (London 1966)

Dalzel, Archibald *The History of Dahomy* (London 1793)

Farwell, Byron *Burton* (London 1963)

Forbes, Frederick E. *Dahomey and the Dahomans* (London 1851)

Greenidge, C. W. W. *Slavery* (London 1958)

Herskovits, M. J. *Dahomey. An Ancient West African Kingdom* (New York 1938)

Mannix, D. P. and Cowley, M. *Black Cargoes* (London 1963)

Newbury, C. W. *The Western Slave Coast and its Rulers* (London 1961)

Norris, R. *Memoirs of the Reign of Bossa Ahadee, King of Dahomey* (London 1789)

Oliver, Caroline *Richard Burton: The African Years* in *Africa and its Explorers* ed. by Robert I. Rotberg (London and Harvard 1970)

Polanyi, Karl *Dahomey and the Slave Trade* (Washington 1966)

Pope-Hennessy, James *Sins of the Fathers* (London 1967)

Skertchly, J. A. *Dahomey As It Is* (London 1874)

Wilson, J. Leighton *The British Squadron on the Coast of Africa* (London 1851)

The Kingdom of Lesotho

Arbousset, T. *Narrative of an Exploratory Tour to the North East of the Colony of the Cape of Good Hope* (London 1852)

Ashton, Hugh *The Basuto. A Social Study of Traditional and Modern Lesotho* (London 1967)

Becker, P. *Hill of Destiny* (London 1969)

Brownlee, the Hon. Charles *Reminiscences of Kaffir Life and History* (Lovedale, South Africa 1896)

Bryce, James *Impressions of South Africa* (London 1898)

Casalis, Eugene *The Basuto* (London 1861)
    My Life in Basutoland (London 1889)

Cory, G. E. *The Rise of South Africa* (London 1921)

Ellenberger, D. F. *History of the Basuto Ancient and Modern* (London 1912)

Lagden, Sir Godfrey *The Basutos* (London 1909)

Molema, S. M. *The Bantu* (Edinburgh 1920)

Oxford History of South Africa Vol. 1 (London 1969)

Rosslyn, Earl of *Twice Captured* (London 1900)

Theal, G. M. *Basutoland Records* (Cape Town 1883)
    History of South Africa Vols III, IV and V (London 1889, 1893)

Thompson, George *Travels and Adventures in Southern Africa* (Cape Town, 1967)

Tylden, G. *The Rise of the Basuto* (Cape Town 1950)
    The History of Thaba Bosiu (Maseru 1945)

Walker, E. A. *The Great Trek* (London 1934)
    A History of South Africa (London 1928)

Worsley, P. *The Trumpet Shall Sound* (London 1957)

Index